MW01713933

Interactive Cases for Business English

edited by

Anne E. Witte

Contributors: *Liz Borredon*
Christine Coisne
Marcus Hurt
Stephanie Hurt
Kevin Jackson
Anne E. Witte

ellipses

ACKNOWLEDGEMENTS

The authors extend grateful thanks to the following persons who kindly contributed to the creation of this book in diverse and useful ways:

Valerie BONELLI, Assistant, Center for Languages and International Communication, Group EDHEC Nice
Marcus HURT, Professor of Strategy, Group EDHEC, Lille
Fabienne LABBE, Assistant, Center for Languages and International Communication, Group EDHEC Lille
Daniel LESCEUX, Professor of Marketing Group EDHEC, Nice
and HABITAT for their kind cooperation.

A big thank you also goes to students at Group EDHEC whose high standards and lofty ambitions set the groundwork for these activities.

An earlier draft of the chapter «Starting a New Company» was published in the Journal of Language for International Business (Phoenix, Arizona) in June 1999.

Bodegas Caballé is also available as a management case with the Centrale des Cas, Paris.

Some of the illustrations and cartoons used in this workbook were drawn from CLICK ART under a licensing agreement.

Any similarity between those materials and actual persons is completely unintentional.

Also published by Ellipses:
Anne E. Witte, *Interactive Business English*, 1997.

ISBN 2-7298-6936-0

© Ellipses Édition Marketing S.A., 1999
32, rue Bargue 75740 Paris cedex 15

DANGER LE PHOTOCOPILLAGE TUE LE LIVRE

Le Code de la propriété intellectuelle n'autorisant, aux termes de l'article L.122-5.2° et 3°a), d'une part, que les « copies ou reproductions strictement réservées à l'usage privé du copiste et non destinées à une utilisation collective », et d'autre part, que les analyses et les courtes citations dans un but d'exemple et d'illustration, « toute représentation ou reproduction intégrale ou partielle faite sans le consentement de l'auteur ou de ses ayants droit ou ayants cause est illicite » (Art. L.122-4).
Cette représentation ou reproduction, par quelque procédé que ce soit constituerait une contrefaçon sanctionnée par les articles L. 335-2 et suivants du Code la propriété intellectuelle.

TABLE OF CONTENTS

CHAPTER DESCRIPTION

1. Habitat

Working in small groups, students piece together information that enables them to respond to a challenging business situation professionally. They make competitive product and/or company presentations which are filmed and they receive constructive feedback from their tutor and from their peers. Personal learning targets are continually assessed.

2. Starting a New Company

This unit requires students to analyze the feasibility of a new company. Carried out in groups of four students working in teams, it aims at building internet research skills, reading between the lines, brainstorming and critical reasoning. Presented with three fictional entrepreneurs as well as possible company start-ups, students take on the role of consultant to assess the outcome of the different ventures that are proposed.

3. MaxiFemme-Ecce Homo

This case study deals with a merger between two clothing manufacturing retailers. The case touches on human resources issues, corporate culture, public relations, company structure and advertising. Among the suggested activities, students write professional documents while creating and then presenting a restructuring plan for a new company.

4. Bodegas Caballé

By reviewing the applications of four potential candidates for an international position, students develop skills in decision-making recruitment policy and the intercultural dimension of recruitment. Working in groups, in pairs and as a class, students continually challenge assumptions and seek maximum objectivity in the selection process. The exercises also develop writing and organisational skills.

5. Van Haffner Toys

This unit requires students to use accounting vocabulary in context. It introduces the main financial statements needed to describe company performance and leads students through a step-by-step analysis of a company's financial situation. By acquiring key accounting and banking terms, students can improve their language skills in dealing with complex financial data.

6. McCarthy's Nickel and Dime Store

Working from the model of the old American «general store,» students consider how merchandising, price policy, location and client profile can be creatively combined to ensure lasting customer loyalty. Creating new opportunities by careful analysis of old problems, students use statistics, charts and graphs to assess a store's future potential.

Answer Key and Glossary

The answer key only contains solutions to the short answer application exercises. The glossary provided at the end of the book is limited to items used in this manual. Each entry is followed by a short French translation and when possible, a second meaning is given for words that may present certain ambiguities. These lists can be used as vocabulary primers for students.

TO THE TEACHER

This manual has been devised for upper-intermediate and advanced students of English and focuses on developping oral communication skills in the classroom. It is particularly suitable for those preparing business degrees, but can be used for programs in Applied Foreign Languages or for in-house company training. Lessons have been designed to resolve the problem of limited speaking time imparted to students in large classes (15-30 students), however, the units can be easily adapted to groups varying from 4 to 40 persons.

One of the main objectives of this material is to improve spontaneity in spoken English by placing students in authentic business situations and requiring participants to formulate complex ideas in the target language. The manual supplements a core EFL/ESL curriculum by concentrating primarily on oral skills and using writing and reading for reinforcement. As with all methods, these materials make several assumptions that would be worthwhile stating.

RATIONALE

The interactive class is an effective means to increase the frequency with which students speak. By exchanging information with peers, as well as with the teacher, students gain confidence and learning becomes centered on their spontaneous communication needs. Objectives for progress are continually assessed.

These lessons focus on integrating the precise use of technical vocabulary, but spontaneity, versatility and confidence building are the overall objectives of this methodology. Aside from concentrating on perfecting the technical aspects of students' discourse, the teacher will obtain greater results from these activities if the focus is on coaching students towards getting the message across in the time and the space constraints given with the greatest accuracy and verbal skill.

The case method also allows interdisciplinary teachers to integrate management training concepts within the language arena. This obliges students to consistently upgrade their language skills as they advance in their technical training. By compelling students to express more and more complex structures and analyses, the cases solicit a range of possible problem-solving contexts that most language teachers will find inducive to intensive language workouts.

This manual is not intended to be a complete English course and is best used as a supplement. Formal grammar, syntax, pronunciation and basic vocabulary building are to be dealt with and followed up in some other context.

The materials provide considerable resources for animating class discussion, writing exercises, and self-study. If used integrally, these units contain learning strategies for more than 30 class hours.

The book comprises six chapters of unequal length. For each chapter, the types of activity and content focus are varied in order to provide for extremely diverse communication simulations. The teacher's introduction indicates the size of the group recommended for most tasks. Although the length of time spent doing the exercises wil vary from teacher to teacher, a general framework for class time is provided on the opening page of each unit.

The pedagogical overview found on the first page of each chapter is intended as a model which teachers will use according to their own needs. It outlines the objectives, methods, preparation and class plan for each case and can be shared with the students if useful. Some chapters also contain an additional set of application exercises which are briefly explained to the teacher. The teacher's page concludes with a suggestion for debriefing.

The student pages contain a variety of tasks, exercises, reading activities and simulations explained in simple language. Space is provided in some exercises so that students can write directly in their own workbook. However, other tasks require students to submit work on separate paper.

Some application exercises have been supplemented with an answer key, but only for vocabulary items. Most tasks require to verify content information within the scope of their management training materials. The purpose of the exercises is to focus on accurate use of technical vocabulary by building on students' confidence and reinforcing correct usage. The subjects for these units have been chosen specifically because they elicit many different problem-solving solutions depending on the audience making it impossible to provide a complete answer key which would encompass this variety.

The glossary found at the end of the book lists only items used in this manual. Each entry is followed by a short French translation and a second meaning is given for words that may present certain ambiguities. Priority is given to the meanings most relevant to usage in this manual.

TO THE STUDENT

Interactive Cases for Business English was designed for business school students and adult learners seeking a challenge in their language of study. The book is intended as a supplement to the more structured learning objectives defined in grammar, vocabulary and business English books.

This manual is about communicating complex ideas in business situations and gaining confidence in spoken English. It assumes that you are committed to language learning and are ready for a challenge.

It also assumes that at least half of your future business contacts in English will be with other non-native speakers of English and that you will need to rapidly gain a certain level of fluency and versatility in English. An important element of the method used will be your involvement in speaking English with members of your class, even if there are no native English speakers among you. You will obtain the best results if you participate actively and are as creative and spontaneous as possible during simulations. The more you contribute, the more you will get out of this workout.

The content ranges from starting a new company, to making presentations, recruiting overseas personnel, analyzing company mergers, interpreting financial statements and much more. It is a good opportunity to use what you've learned elsewhere and express it in accurate and fluent English.

Activities will be carried out in pairs, in groups and in plenary sessions. Space has been provided in most exercises for you to write your answers directly in this book. Research assignments and homework will allow all participants to consider the problem-solving dimension of cases per individual needs.

Chapter one and chapter five have been prepared using British style, spelling and punctuation. The other chapters adapt American conventions. You should utilize one spelling convention and stick to it. Mixing spellings in writing assignments gives a confused impression.

A model teacher's plan has been provided at the start of each chapter and will allow you to anticipate what will be going on. At the end of this book, a glossary has been provided which gives translations for most business vocabulary items used. It would be useful from time to time to test your vocabulary skills by taking one letter per day and making sure you have mastered all of the words listed.

Chapter 1

The Habitat Catalogue Competition

Case Concept and Exercises

by

Liz Borredon

360 min.

HABITAT CATALOGUE COMPETITION
Lesson Overview

LANGUAGE OBJECTIVES

To consolidate and practice the vocabulary used in product presentations
To demonstrate previously acquired marketing, distribution or business know-how in fluent and professional English
To make a convincing and inspiring presentation

MANAGERIAL OBJECTIVES

To strategically position a product or service
To develop creativity in team situations
To evaluate performance according to personal learning objectives
To give and receive constructive feedback

PEDAGOGICAL NOTES

The HABITAT Catalogue Competition is designed for students with some business experience. The case accommodates from 15 to 30 participants and requires a minimum of 6 hours of class time over three separate lessons. Students will need to devote preparation time to this case between classes. The case necessitates the use of a video camera in order to film presentations. A TV monitor and video recorder are needed in the final lessons.

While presentations are made in groups, individual feedback is given when debriefing performance. After the presentations, the class brainstorms criteria for effective presentations in order to draw up guidelines for improvement.

DEBRIEFING

After the selection panel has completed its presentation, the instructor conducts a 30 minute debriefing of the recorded performance separately with each group. In order to maximise learning, feedback on vocabulary, use of language, fluency, group dynamics and professionalism are taken into account. Reviewing the filmed performance is an opportunity to stand back from personal performance and have an objective appraisal of progress. As the debriefing takes place in sub-groups, students constructively critique peers and in the process, develop skill in giving feedback as opposed to making judgmental statements.

HABITAT CATALOGUE COMPETITION
Application Exercises

DIRECTIONS FOR EXERCISE 1

As you work through this chapter and attend different presentations, keep a record of the different criteria for a successful presentation.

CRITERIA FOR SUCCESSFUL PRESENTATIONS

DIRECTIONS FOR EXERCISE 2

In this case, you will work in small groups to prepare for a professional presentation, deliver it and then review your own performance. The case permits you to maximise previously acquired skills and develop your capacity to use them in promoting or selecting a product or service.

The exhibits that follow contain all the data you need for piecing together information about the HABITAT Catalogue Competition. When you have read these documents, follow the instructions for preparing your role.

HABITAT CATALOGUE COMPETITION
Exhibit 1

ATTENTION PRODUCT INNOVATORS!

Compete in our annual

HABITAT CATALOGUE COMPETITION

IF
you provide excellence, quality & innovation
AND
you convince us that you are the best in your field
THEN
you can be included in the

HABITAT 2002 CATALOGUE

Paper or disc submissions must reach our London Offices by December 15th of this year

A short-list will be communicated in February

Those short-listed will be allowed 20 minutes to present their product or service to our panel

Final selection will take place in April

The panel's choice is final

Habitat Catalogue Competition/Box 3456/Bowling Green/
London/WX 1YZ3
wannahabitat@comf.net

HABITAT CATALOGUE COMPETITION
Exhibit 2

HIGH FLYERS AND INNOVATORS

The Professional Journal for Creative People

HABITAT CATALOGUE COMPETITION 2002 LAUNCHED!

Simon Macquark

Habitat's claim that a constant stream of suppliers knock on their doors in the hope of attracting attention to the product or service they have carefully reared for an increasingly capricious consumer market has led the company to adopt a new selection strategy. With unceasing dedication to provide no less than quality innovation whether in traditional or high tech design, Habitat has decided on a new approach for identifying high flyers. They did not call for tender, they called for creative talent. Their medium? A Catalogue Competition.

The Habitat chain launched their competition earlier this year and it is proving to be an outstanding success. "*We are overwhelmed by the quality of innovative responses to our recent challenge to innovators,*" says a Habitat spokesperson who added, "*We are determined to enforce our drive and enhance the firm's image as a provider of quality and innovation in the new millennium*".

Finalists, Tracey Smarts and Bob Practical, prepare for the April competition.

Some detective work on the part of our press team reveals that Habitat's selection panel has already been nominated and while we as yet have no criteria for selection procedures, we are told that total quality customer service, and rigorous product specification will be at the forefront together with feasibility of after-sales provision, guarantees and attractive pricing.

As never before, Habitat turns up trumps! Their search for high- flyers is taking off in a big way...

SOME FACTS ABOUT HABITAT

1600 Employees and 40 stores in the UK
Branches in France, Luxembourg, Spain, Germany, Greece, Italy, Portugal, Thailand, and Belgium.

HABITAT CATALOGUE COMPETITION
Exhibit 3

BAYLISS ENTERPRISES

MEMO

From Fred Bayliss
To R&D Units Bayliss Enterprises
Subject HABITAT 2002 COMPETITION
Date 3 November ____

You have my go-ahead to submit for the HABITAT Catalogue Competition. I need four suggestions from our R&D units.

Each unit should work independently. Use all your know-how in designing a presentation that does us credit. Strive for excellence. Maintain the competitive edge between yourselves as this will enhance performance. One team will win but we must ensure that this winner also attains national selection and that Bayliss Enterprises gains a prestigious place in the HABITAT 2002 Catalogue. Decide on who is best qualified to promote your chosen product or indeed service.

We cannot afford to fail!

While we have a variety of products and services on offer, we are still in further competition with Hanger and Sprigg, Singleton Options and EternityNet who have already been nominated for the final stage of the competition.

I am determined that we remain both innovative and competitive with an insatiable appetite for progress. To this end, I shall conduct a detailed debriefing after Bayliss Enterprises has presented to the selection-panel. Ensure your presentation objectives are clearly recorded in order that we are able to review and compare notes effectively after the event.

N.B.:Enclosed photocopy from recent HABITAT catalogue which is inspiring material.

HABITAT CATALOGUE COMPETITION
Exhibit 4

Telephone conversation between:
Stanley Oberfield - HABITAT Communication Consultant
Alice Stoops - HABITAT Catalogue Promotions Manager

Stanley	*Hi Alice, things seem to be moving at an incredible pace round there. I tried to get you yesterday on the selection panel job, but was told I had no hope of catching you before this morning.*
Alice	*Hi Stan, I've just read your e-mail but haven't got 'round to responding, sorry about that.*
Stanley	*No problem! What's happening?*
Alice	*Entrants have been coming in thick and fast. We have reached the deadline so we are no longer accepting any other suppliers. As you say, we must give priority to establishing who is on the panel. What are the instructions from above?*
Stanley	*Much the same as last week. We really want to go for a new image in the next issue and certainly don't want a hum drum approach to selection. Can we get some of those new people in there?*
Alice	*You mean the two from Goldsmiths?*
Stanley	*Yes, can you include them with one or two from the old brigade?*
Alice	*You bet! I am getting inspired about this panel. I think we should go for a mixed bunch and avoid favouring any one section. How long do I get?*
Stanley	*Till yesterday!*
Alice	*Heavens, that sounds like the boss talking.*
Stanley	*I was only half kidding, we can't hang around on this. Your suggestion of a mixed panel is not really what I had in mind, let me mull it over and I'll get back to you.*
Alice	*OK Stan, I get the message. We'll work on identifying potential and as soon as you give the go ahead, I'll inform section heads and get the team together.*
Stanley	*Great stuff Alice, I know its been hectic but we'll make it yet!*
Alice	*Thanks for the encouragement!*
Stanley	*See you!*

HABITAT CATALOGUE COMPETITION
Exhibit 5

oberfield communications

Stanley Oberfield, Consultant
West Greenwich WC2334 London
oberfield@net.en

London New York Milan Brussels Paris Barcelona Berlin

FACSIMILE

From	Stanley Oberfield Communications Consultant	1 PAGE
To	Alice Stoops HABITAT Catalogue Promotions	
Re	Catalogue 2002	
Date	1 December _____	

Alice,

I have been thinking over our recent call. You are right, we need to have a varied panel. Go ahead and ask for people from Textiles, Interiors, Furniture, Glass and Ceramics and Customer Services. Don't get back to me until you are ready to give me the names.

Have fun!

Stan

HABITAT CATALOGUE COMPETITION
Application Exercises

DIRECTIONS FOR EXERCISE 3

The class divides into five groups. Four groups of students work for Bayliss Enterprises, the fifth group works for HABITAT.

Bayliss Enterprises Product Innovation Team: Each of the four groups is in competition with the three other groups from the same firm. During this session, you will design, adapt or choose a product or service to be presented to the HABITAT selection panel. In order to plan your presentation, you will continue preparing with your peers until the next class session.

Remember that creativity in adopting a product is only one aspect of this exercise. Seek out information on HABITAT as a source of enrichment and added value.

When you have identified your good or service, work on designing your presentation. Consider what type of support or illustrative material you will need.

Allocate a role to each member of your group and ensure that you attribute equal speaking time among you.

Dress for the occasion. Decide on the degree of formality you consider appropriate for a professional presentation.

The HABITAT selection panel: You establish the criteria for selecting a product or service for the HABITAT 2002 Catalogue and you outline priorities. Acting as facilitator and welcoming participants, you ensure each presentation is limited to 20 minutes and announce the results at the end.

Design your selection procedure. Prepare appropriate vocabulary, allocate roles for each member of your group as well as equal speaking time. You will need to consider what type of support material is appropriate and prepare accordingly.

You will be creating a HABITAT environment. Consider how the room should be set up and how to dress for the occasion.

HABITAT CATALOGUE COMPETITION
Application Exercises

DIRECTIONS FOR EXERCISE 4

This exercise may either be done in class or for homework. It will help you to overcome some of language difficulties when making presentations. Use one of the following words or phrases in the gaps provided. A word might need to be used more than once. Some words will not be used at all.

When you have completed this task, consider the verbs used in the exercise and suggest an alternative in each case.

to present to deal with to introduce to explain to take to divide to overstate to criticise to aspire to to sustain to capture to bear in mind to tell to say	objective concerns loyalty date issues purpose introducing presenting experience experiment subject deadline delivery loss leader part persuasive suggestion pricing counterfeits	you his	how on to for in after	the

1. I will now introduce __________ __________ of my presentation.

2. After __________ members of our team, we __________ __________ our objectives.

3. Mark has just __________ __________ pricing strategy. Let's move __________ __________ the second part of our presentation.

HABITAT CATALOGUE COMPETITION
Application Exercises

4. We would like to explain _________ the table is assembled.

5. Customer _________ is one of our main _________ .

6. There will be more time for questions at a later _________ .

7. We have _________ with a number of _________ during this presentation. It might now be useful to _________ _________ for delivery before closing.

8. Habitat does not favour _________ pricing. Our design _________ _________ into account. HABITAT's _________ for quality and fair _________ throughout the store.

9. We have _________ our presentation into four _________ .

10. We have not _________ our merits, neither have we _________ competitive products. We have presented the merits of our service which we firmly believe correspond to the quality _________ _________ by HABITAT.

11. You really _________ our attention with a very _________ message.

12. Let us begin by _________ the importance of environmentally safe raw materials and the life cycle of the biodegradable components of this prototype.

13. Clearly HABITAT does not compete with DIY stores, and we do not have the problem of _________ . Nevertheless they must _________ the _________ market _________ mind.

14. We need to look _________ all our interests.

15. My colleague has just _________ _________ about our production procedures. He _________ that we are open to _________ regarding finishes.

HABITAT CATALOGUE COMPETITION
Application Exercises

DIRECTIONS FOR EXERCISE 5

1. Consider the type of language used in the telephone conversation between Stanley Oberfield and Alice Stoops.

2. What does this conversation tell you about their work context and corporate culture?

3. How would you identify Stanley Oberfield's management style?

4. What other management styles are there?

5. In pairs, conduct another conversation adopting the register which would indicate a different management style or a different corporate context.

6. When all pairs have experimented with different communication styles, the group listens to some of the pairs working through their conversations. After each conversation, the teacher comments on choice of register.

DIRECTIONS FOR EXERCISE 6

Bayliss Enterprises Product Innovation Team:

You make presentations of not more than 20 minutes and respond to questions asked by the panel, or other competitors. All presentations are filmed by a facilitator.

HABITAT Selection Panel:

You manage the presentations, arrange the room, welcome product innovators, and ensure groups keep to time. A facilitator will film your brief introductory speech. You also need to handle questions from participants. Make sure that you use your selection criteria throughout the presentations, you will need to refer to these observations when you present your findings.

HABITAT CATALOGUE COMPETITION
Application Exericses

DIRECTIONS FOR EXERCISE 8

The HABITAT Selection Panel: You present your findings to the class. You explain selection criteria and then analyse each of the products accordingly. You present your final choice of product or service to be included in a future final round of the HABITAT 2002 catalogue competition. This presentation is also filmed.

DIRECTIONS FOR EXERCISE 9

Read the press cutting again. Discuss the written style. The class divides into groups of four participants. Two write a brief article announcing the winner of the competition. You adopt a similar style to the press cutting in exhibit 2. Two write a brief article announcing the winner of the competition. You adopt a very different style to the press cutting in exhibit 2

DIRECTIONS FOR EXERCISE 10

All partipants prepare for the debriefing by drawing up a list of the different criteria which determine a successful presentation.

HABITAT CATALOGUE COMPETITION
Bibliography

The following materials have proven useful in preparing this case and may help readers go further with class materials. The version presented in this document has been tailored for a general audience involved in business and needing to communicate with professional presentations. The case can also be adapted to a problem-based learning context with the objective to induce critical analysis of what constitutes a good presentation as well as of assessing product innovation in a market driven society.

Aranda,E.K., Aranda, L., with Conlon,K., 1998., *Teams: structure, process, culture, and politics,* New Jersey, Prentice Hall.

Comfort, J., & Brieger, N., 1992., *Marketing*, Business Management English, London, Prentice Hall International.

Barker,L.L., 1990., *Communication,* New Jersey, Prentice Hall.

De Vito, J.A., 1993., *Essentials of Human Communication,* New York, Harper Collins.

Guirdham, M., 1990., *Interpersonal Skills at Work,* Hertfordshire, Prentice Hall.

Henninger Chiang, T., & Reel, J., 1998., *Professional Presentations: how to succeed in international business,* The University of Michigan Press.

Kotler, P., 1997., *Marketing Management,* New Jersey, Prentice Hall International.

Munter, M., 1997., *Guide to MANAGERIAL COMMUNICATION: Effective Business Writing and Speaking,* NJ, Prentice Hall.

Witte, A.E., 1997., *Interactive Business English,* Paris, Ellipses.

The author extends warmest appreciation to HABITAT for the permission to use their brand name and talk about their catalogue in this chapter.

Chapter 2

Starting a New Company

Case Concept and Exercises

by

Anne E. Witte

360 min.

STARTING A NEW COMPANY
Lesson Overview

LANGUAGE OBJECTIVES

To acquire the vocabulary related to the different kinds of businesses, loans, and investment
To structure a report based on research with an aim to convince by introducing legal, financial and market evidence
To condense a written report into a short professional presentation

MANAGERIAL OBJECTIVES

To consider different start-up options for small investors
To conduct research on loan prospects for new business
To weigh different business proposals and choose a potential winner
To forecast market trends

PEDAGOGICAL NOTES

Students read the case in class with the instructor and the language and managerial objectives are carefully explained. In groups of three to four, students prepare their analysis outside of class. Each group must defend one of the proposed projects. Their conclusions are presented before an audience of 9-15 students and all of the reports are debriefed in full group. During the reports, three students chosen at random play the roles of the people for whom the report is intended. They should challenge assumptions and ask informed questions. It is usually beneficial for the students if the entire written report is corrected and handed back before the oral presentation.

DEBRIEFING

Depending on the level of the students and the amount of outside work feasible for them, the conclusion of the course can be more or less managerial or language oriented. The content debriefing may inspire research on the laws regarding start-ups in the US, the European Community and, for example, China. It may also involve checking country laws regarding loans and financial aid to new businesses specifying the types of activity which are particularly encouraged. This information is covered in most textbooks on entrepreneurship and can be found in a general business library. For the forecast information, students will need to draw primarily from the press and also from similar company histories. In this part, the teacher should concentrate on reviewing with students strategies for finding information. The wrap-up can be made by drawing up the feasibility criteria for starting a new company.

STARTING A NEW COMPANY
Case Background

Patricia Kern, Walter Chapman and Peter Johnson Timo have been friends since they studied together at the State University of California. Although they have not been able to maintain regular contact due to geographic distances and professional obligations, they have kept in touch and generally get together once a year every summer.

The reunion this year proved to be a turning point in all of their lives. Patricia, who was appointed as an Accounting teacher in 1990 at a community college near her home, felt boredom with her job which lacked prospects. Walter, father of two children, had just divorced and was considering a career move from his public relations and advertising job within a large publishing company. Peter, who was a free lance writer, translator and anthropologist, had become restless and felt his creative talents were still untapped.

It occurred to the three friends that pooling their energies and talents by setting up a new business might be a solution for them all. After all, a year sabbatical for Walter and Patricia was negotiable with their employers to whom they had given several loyal years of service. Peter, a free spirit anyway, had flexibility in his schedule. They gave themselves a year after which they could all assess the situation and make a long-term decision.

The group brainstormed several ideas on start-ups. These included:

an export business in holiday decorations (Halloween, Christmas, birthdays etc.) destined for Europe

a consultancy service for medium-sized businesses specializing in cultural issues, language and translation

an internet-based company which sold products to aging baby-boomers: old albums, photos, interviews, rare news pieces, memorabilia from the Vietnam war era and the 1960's

an on-line business consultancy service offering expert advice in cultural issues, fund-raising and humanitarian causes

an import business specializing in European upmarket household decorations

a publishing company dealing in reprints of rare, hard-to-find illustrated books on travel, geography and human geography

STARTING A NEW COMPANY
Case Background

Since they lacked experience in entrepreneurship and wished to have an outside opinion on their future venture, they decided to hire a group of independent consultants to help them evaluate their prospects and eventually work out a strategy. The consultants' mission was:

to study the feasibility of each start-up prospect and/or other likely prospects and decide which one was worth the investment

to audit each individual's financial and professional capabilities

to draw up a working model of the new company stating each person's duties as well as the capital and resources necessary for launching

to investigate and identify sources of outside financing

to designate the place, context and framework in which the company could be created

to identify risks and opportunities by comparing this business with similar known business concerns

to analyze all of the legal implications

Because the three were willing to take a risk at this point in their lives, they specified the following:

they had no geographic restrictions within or outside the US

the company could be virtual, mail-order, shop, or office

all three were willing to perform whatever duties necessary

all were willing to provide an initial cash investment amounting to $100,000

STARTING A NEW COMPANY ASSIGNMENT

You are an outside consultant called in to run the audit. Consider all of the material listed in the case as well as the personal interview notes provided by an independent headhunter and the *curricula vitae* given on the following pages (exhibits 1-6).

1. Draw up a six page report to defend one recommendation for the final start-up. It needs to outline what the three people should do (considering market opportunity and feasibility) not what they can do. The report should include relevant annexes such as statistics, addresses, forms to fill out, loan information etc. The report should be as practical as possible and presented for a non-specialist. It should include suggestions and forecasts for every aspect of the chosen future company: projected sales, expected costs, internal organization, distribution, insurance, legal aid etc. Textbooks on entrepreneurship and your local business reference library should provide most of the necessary information.

2. Present the main points in a fifteen minute presentation.

3. Leave your detailed bill at the end of the meeting.

You will be evaluated on the following criteria:

Research endeavor

Accuracy of vocabulary

Grammatical precision

Argumentation and persuasiveness

Feasibility

Structure and coherence of the report

Presentation skills

STARTING A NEW COMPANY
Exhibit 1

RESUME
Patricia Kern

EDUCATION

1982 MSc in Accounting and Finance
The State University of California

1978 BS Business Administration
Minor in Chinese
The State University of California

WORK EXPERIENCE

1992 to the present
Professor of Accounting and Finance, San Diego Community College
San Diego Community College is a diverse two year university program with over 15000 students
Senior staff member responsible for all courses in accounting
Faculty representative
Tutor for 20 students
Creator of a self-learning tutorial in reading and analyzing balance sheets
Participant in a local think tank on San Diego business

1986-1992
Richard Seaway Inc. Assistant Financial Director
Richard Seaway is an investment group specializing in Asian stock
Audited subsidiaries throughout California
Established companies' yearly earnings reviews
Set up a cost accounting plan for companies with more than 20 employees
Assisted the Financial Director

1982-1986
Globetrotters Publishing. General Office Manager
Globetrotters is a small publishing company specialized in Orientalia.
Managed front and back offices
Assisted the Chief Editor in Market Strategy
Kept the books

SKILLS

Familiar with finance software
Speak some Mandarin
Excellent knowledge of California and Maryland business law

STARTING A NEW COMPANY
Exhibit 2

HEADLESS HEADHUNTERS
A Human Resources Consultancy Group

Personal Information

Patricia Kern
Residing presently in Baltimore, Maryland
Single, 42 years old
Solvent up to $50,000
Some savings, no current investments

Interests

Orientalia
Traveling
Memorabilia 1960's

Patricia Kern
September 1999

INTERVIEWER'S COMMENTS

Patricia Kern is a practical woman of average intelligence. Bored with her life, she is seeking something different for the second half of her career. She is not particularly creative, but an excellent teamworker who is willing to follow orders and implement other people's ideas.

White, middle-class. Never married because «she never found the right situation.»

Owns a duplex apartment and a 1997 Ford Mondeo.

Spends free time in public lectures, in museums and listening to 60's music.

Impressive technical experience in financial analysis and managerial accounting.

STARTING A NEW COMPANY
Exhibit 3

RESUME
Walter Chapman

EDUCATION

1982 MBA Master of Business Administration
The State University of California

1978 BA Bachelor of Arts and Applied Arts
Minor in Chinese
The State University of California

WORK EXPERIENCE

1989 to the present
Moughton Publishers
Senior Advertising and Public Relations Manager
Moughton Publishers employs 1500 people worldwide and is specialized in atlases, geography, tourism, area studies and civilization.
manage 20 full time advertising and marketing professionals
wrote copy for over 50 illustrated documents this year
published worldwide
oversee the European branches
participate in the overall strategy of the firm

1988-1989
Craft and Croft, Inc. Sales Director
Craft and Croft is a mail order company specialized in kitchenware
wrote sales copy for catalogue
planned catalogue specials
organized creative team

1982-1988
In His Hands, Assistant Public Relations Manager
In His Hands is a humanitarian association aimed at generating financial aid for hungry children throughout the world
identified fund raising opportunities throughout the West Coast
organized direct mail shots
wrote advertising and TV copy
participated in the 1985 World Hunger Project in Africa

SKILLS

Speak fluent Spanish and an authority on Spanish literature after 1945

STARTING A NEW COMPANY
Exhibit 4

HEADLESS HEADHUNTERS
A Human Resources Consultancy Group

Personal Information
Walter Chapman
Resides in Kalamazoo, Michigan
44 years old
divorced, two children
Solvent up to $500,000
Investments, savings and bonds

Interests
Hiking
Chess
Painting and Drawing

Walter Chapman
September 1999

INTERVIEWER'S COMMENTS

Walter Chapman is known and respected in the publishing field where he earns a handsome salary. His employment history has been mostly stable and he does have opportunities to be promoted within his present job, but his recent divorce has upset his well being. Feeling the need to return to the passions of his youth, he is searching for meaning in his life and is prepared to leave the comforts of what he has attained to commit his time to something satisfying and enduring before he grows old.

White, upper-middle class. Aspires to re-marry quickly.

Has always been financially stable, but now must pay alimony for his wife and children.

Owns a large house in a well-to-do residential area, but his wife and children will remain there indefinitely. Drives a BMW.

Spends his free time painting and drawing. Attends art classes at night. Articulate, professional and personable. A good sense for PR.

STARTING A NEW COMPANY
Exhibit 5

RESUME
Peter Johnson Timo

EDUCATION

1986 **Ph.D** in Applied Anthropology and Linguistics
The State University of California
Thesis Topic: Tracing American Indian Languages to Prehistoric Asia - New Perspectives in Methodology
Grade Point Average 3.8

1982 **MA**, Master of Arts in General Anthropology and Linguistics

1978 **BA** French/Italian/Spanish
Minor in Chinese
The State University of California

WORK EXPERIENCE

1986 to the present, Free-lance consultant

Projects have included:

1. The State University of California vs the Hanhuan Indian Tribes

   provided expert information about the Hanhuans
   led negotiations concerning zoning laws
   translated witnesses' statements in court
   published an article in *American Anthropologist* on this case

2. Sonia Music Distributor's campaign in Los Angeles

   advised foreign distributors about American cultural practices
   assisted strategical team with administrative procedures for company set-up
   planned a public relations campaign
   learned basic Japanese

3. Translated a contemporary French sociologist's novel into English: *Remembrance of Things Present.* Published in 1993

STARTING A NEW COMPANY
Exhibit 5 (cont)

RESUME
Peter Johnson Timo

WORK EXPERIENCE (Cont.)

4. Acted as a private consultant for the Guggenforth Museum in New York City

advised public relations team on advertising campaigns
translated brochures into French/Italian/Spanish with a team of specialists
led a multicultural interest group to lobby for diverse exhibits
organized the first Native American contemporary exhibit

5. Fiction and Non-Fiction Published

The Last Days of Driar Harbor, 1996
Six Lessons in Communication Studies, 1995
She Said: Women and the Cultural Revolution in China, 1993
Various articles in *The American Anthropologist*

SKILLS

Language Enthusiast: speak fluent French/Italian/Spanish and strong skills in Mandarin, Japanese and several native American languages.

STARTING A NEW COMPANY
Exhibit 6

HEADLESS HEADHUNTERS
A Human Resources Consultancy Group

Peter Johnson Timo
September 1999

Personal Information

Peter Johnson Timo
Resides in Hoboken, New Jersey
41 years old, Single
Solvent up to $100,000
No investments, savings or collectibles

Interests

Classical Music
Hiking
Ancient History
Geography

INTERVIEWER'S COMMENTS

Peter Johnson Timo is an exceptionally gifted individual. Not only does he speak several languages, he is a competent writer of both fiction and non-fiction and he has limitless artistic abilities. Although bright and energetic, he is not particularly interested in mundane daily business and he is not always reliable when it comes to practical work.

Native American, Latin American and European origins. Never married and has a history of diverse personal relationships.

Earnings have varied throughout the years depending on projects. Rents a comfortable duplex and travels only by public transportation as virtually all of his time outside his workshop is spent in Manhattan.Does not perceive leisure time and work time as being separate. Some describe him as an intellectual snob

STARTING A NEW COMPANY
Application Exercises

DIRECTIONS FOR EXERCISE 1

Role Play: You have just heard the consultant's opinions on what the three partners should do. Play the part of Patricia, Walter and Peter by expressing your thoughts and questions.

DIRECTIONS FOR EXERCISE 2

Brainstorm the essential criteria which need to be considered when starting a new company by indicating each factor under the categories indicated.

CRITERIA FOR STARTING A NEW COMPANY

PARTNERS	TYPES OF BUSINESS	INVESTMENT
MARKET INFO	**LOCATION**	**ENVIRONMENT**
FINANCING	**LEGAL**	**OTHER**

STARTING A NEW COMPANY
Application Exercises

DIRECTIONS FOR EXERCISE 3

Complete the following sentences using the example as a guide for grammatical structure and the case to input content.

Example:
Had we more money, we surely would have bought a better car.

1. Had Walter Chapman's marriage been more successful,______________

____.

2. ______________________________________, it would not have been so difficult to market the item in Europe.

3. Had Internet the same impact in China as it does in the USA,

____.

4. Peter Johnson Timo would have done well in the context of a consultantcy service in cultural issues, language and translation,

____.

5. Patricia Kern would have continued working as a college professor,

____.

6. Had memorabilia been more popular in the southern US,

____.

7. ______________________________________, they could have tried their luck in a less questionable start-up activities.

8. ______________________________________, the costs of exports would have been much lower.

STARTING A NEW COMPANY
Application Exercises

DIRECTIONS FOR EXERCISE 4

Complete the following prompts by using the grammar structure indicated in the example with content information given in the case.

Example:
Either Patricia Kern keeps the books, or you should pay an accountant.

1. Either Walter Chapman moves to ______________________________

____.

2. ______________________________, or he can not truly be considered an equal partner.

3. ______________________________, or the import tax in the European Community will make the product uncompetitive.

4. Either they sign a contract among themselves, ____________________

____.

5. Neither did they tell their relatives, ______________________________

____.

6. Peter Johnson Timo had neither relatives, ____________________ that would have prevented him from moving.

7. In order to be successful in a virtual business, ____________________

____.

8. Either they move to a state with lower sales taxes, ____________________

____.

STARTING A NEW COMPANY
Application Exercises

DIRECTIONS FOR EXERCISE 5

Use the following words to complete the prompts.

judging from these examples	on account of
whereas	in spite of
for the purpose of	thus
obviously	to the extent that

1. Walter Chapman is eager to leave Michigan ____________ his divorce.

2. ____________ tremendous creativity, Peter Johnson Timo may turn out to be an unsuccessful entrepreneur.

3. We conducted a market survey ____________ identifying consumer interest.

4. Patricia Kern won't mind administrative tasks ____________ Peter Johnson Timo will shun them.

5. The initial investment seems sufficient ____________ each start-up requires really only one third of the funds available.

6. Having considered his publication list, we think that Peter is ____________ the most competent to run an intercultural firm.

7. Here is Walter's press book. ____________ he should prove to be an efficient communicator.

8. None of the projects were feasible, ____________ we are proposing a totally new concept.

Chapter 3

Bodegas Caballé

Case Concept and Exercises

by

Stephanie and Marcus Hurt

BODEGAS CABALLE
Lesson Overview

240 min.

LANGUAGE AND MANAGERIAL OBJECTIVES

To analyze and summarize company plans and strategy
To communicate qualifications needed for management and sales positions
To learn to write job offers
To express people's suitability for job assignments
To write reports to top management

METHODS

This exercise can be carried out effectively in groups of up to 30 students. It is best when alternated between small groups and plenary sessions to compare group decisions. Final written work may be done individually or in teams as an in-class exercise, or at home.

By providing the students with credible management material, the exercise enables them to apply vocabulary related to personality traits, work experience, education and job assignments while making an important management decision.

Throughout the exercise the teacher should move from group to group, writing down students' most common difficulties in communication to order to use this information during the debriefing sessions. In the plenary sessions the teacher may usefully play the role of facilitator to write on the board more carefully developed ways of expressing students' ideas.

PREPARATION AND CLASS PLAN

Students should be asked to find examples of recruitment ads in the English press before coming to class. For a 180-minute work-out, the in-class work could be divided into the following phases:

1 In groups of four or five, students analyze the company's commissioning letter and draw up a list of criteria to be used in the selection process. **Exercises 1 through 3 are completed**. During this phase the teacher may work separately with each group to help them word the qualifications in complete and meaningful phrases: *45 minutes.*

BODEGAS CABALLE
Lesson Overview

2 In this phase, students draft a recruiting advertisement for the Central European press based on examples they have collected before class and the preliminary work done in Exercises 1 through 3. **Exercises 4 through 7 are completed.** The final drafts of the job offer may by passed from one group to the other for comparison at the end of this stage: *45 minutes.*

3 **Exercise 8.** Students continue to work in small groups. They now study the four agency recruitment reports and rank the applicants from 1 to 4 with the best candidate ranking 1. This ranking must be done in case their first choice refuses the job. The groups must be ready to defend their choices orally in plenary session: *45 minutes.*

4 In plenary session, the teacher writes the rankings of each group on a flip chart. Then, on the board, the teacher should list the *Assets* and *Liabilities* of each applicant, one by one, as the groups call them out. Debate should be encouraged. This requires the groups to defend their thinking and allows the teacher to work on the vocabulary in order to help the students develop a more enriched wording of their viewpoint about the applicants: *45 minutes.*

5 Exercise 9 is a wrap-up exercise where students are asked to draft a one-page report defending their own recruitment choice. As an alternative, the report might be written calling into question the recruiting agency's original shortlist. In either case, this report will allow students to perfect the phrasing of complex ideas worked out during the in-class sessions. If time permits, **Exercise 9** can be done in class.

DEBRIEFING

Keep as interactive as possible, moving from group to group and focusing students' language on the precise analysis and expression needed in this exercise. Maintain tension by querying students as to what they really mean when they suggest a selection criterion or mention what they consider to be a positive or negative point about an applicant. What might the outcomes of such a strength or weakness be? This will encourage students to develop more complex sentences and wording, and move them from holding mere opinions to extrapolating the effects of choice. In the plenary session, make sure the students are doing the talking, but help them add vocabulary and structures that will enable them to write a sophisticated final report. Keep calling for other groups' input on what one group has expressed.

BODEGAS CABALLE
Application Exercises

PREPARATION: EXERCISE 1

In small groups, read the commissioning letter from *Bodegas Caballé* on the following pages. As you read, exchange opinions on the company, its past, its culture and its strategy and take notes. Ask your teacher to explain difficult passages. *Do <u>NOT</u> read the recruitment reports before you do Exercises 1 through 7.*

DIRECTIONS FOR EXERCISE 1

As a group, work out the selection criteria you feel are most important in choosing a candidate on the heuristic base below. Think of the best way to express each criteria so that a recruiter can clearly understand what you are looking for. Debate among yourselves why you feel these traits, skills and background are important. Work on the vocabulary exercises 2 and 3 to help you fill in the grid below.

ESSENTIAL CRITERIA

____

____

____

____

____

____

DESIRABLE CRITERIA	**WEIGHTING 1-9** (with 9 as most important)

BODEGAS CABALLE
Case Background

Bodegas

Central European Consulting and Recruiting
Ul.Paderewski
Warsaw, Poland

Dear Sirs,

Our associates in Northern Spain have recommended your executive recruitment services. Bodegas Caballé is Spain's leading producer of fine wines with presence in major markets all over the world. Our current strategy aims at developing a position in Central Europe that will lead to important growth in the coming years. For this, our company wishes to commission your agency to recruit a sales representative for Bodegas Caballé for this region. Below I have outlined Company history, strategy and culture, as well as our assessment of Central European opportunities, to enable your consultants to target suitable applicants.

Company history: The original vineyards of the Company have been cultivated by the Caballé family since the 17th Century. Bodegas Caballé itself was founded by Alejandro Caballé in 1875. Until WW1, our wines were bottled for sale on the domestic market but were exported in bulk to markets like the United States, where they were often marketed as simple table wine. However, in the ensuing years, bottling and labeling all output as Bodegas Caballé wine became the rule. In the 30s, the company diversified into the production of brandies.

Recent strategy: Over the last few years, sizable direct investment has been carried out in South America and the U.S. on major land acquisitions, where large-scale vineyards have been planted for production for local markets. Production and distribution is handled by country-specific subsidiaries. In Spain, stress has been laid on the development of high quality 'pagos' wines, which are meant to be more like the French 'cru' wines. This upgrading dovetails with our global move upmarket into higher added value products. This shift has gone hand in hand with efforts to deal directly with major hotel and restaurant chains, rather than going through wines and spirits distributors. Lately, the company has begun selling into less 'traditional markets' such as Germany, Scandinavia, Japan and Australia. An import business of gourmet food products for the Spanish market has also been developed.

Corporate culture: Bodegas Caballé prides itself on being a family business. The Board as well as many subsidiary heads are family members. We feel that wine production is a traditional art based on solid family values. We shun an American-style management approach with its focus on short-term profit and disdain for human values. It has been our policy to keep equity in family hands and avoid alliances or other working relationships with major luxury goods or food groups. However, in the last decade an increasing number of business school graduates have been brought in and have taken part in re-engineering a certain number of operations and revamping accounting and stock management systems. The growing complexity and competitiveness of the environment have made it necessary to 'professionalize' the business. Yet, despite the need for non wine-business track records, we have often experienced difficulty in fitting people from professional management backgrounds into our wine-technology centered culture. Our driving values have become «innovation, intuition, hard steady work, and loyalty.»

BODEGAS CABALLE
Case Background

Central Europe: Our market research shows that the boom in sales of Hungarian and Bulgarian wines that followed the fall of the old regimes is over. Sales of commodity-type wines have been eroded by pressure from French and Californian wines, which benefit from a Western life-style image and cosmopolitan reputation. However, such wines demand premium prices. We feel the outlook is good for high-quality wines of similar renown at lower prices. Our objectives for this area in the medium term are, in the following order:

- ➡ Develop significant market presence for Bodegas Caballé on the Polish market, which seems the most receptive to Western consumption habits. Make major inroads for the brand with the fast-growing French and German hypermarket chains in the country.
- ➡ Set up a company subsidiary and train a sales team to expand sales into restaurants, hotels and specialty shops.
- ➡ Develop a market for our gourmet foods.
- ➡ Develop a marketing strategy for all of Central Europe and make the brand name known in capitals like Prague and Budapest.

We hope this provides sufficient insight into our company and goals to enable you to draw up a profile and shortlist a number of high-potential candidates to forward to our offices. Starting yearly compensation will be in the $45,000 to $60,000 range plus negotiable commission. Final recruitment will be made by an in-house Selection Committee. We will need full files on the candidates within 2 months time.

Please contact me if you need any other information before that time.

Yours sincerely,

Mauricio Caballé

Mauricio Caballé
Presidente

Bodegas Caballé

Head Office 16 Avenida Antonio Gaudi, Barcelona, Spain
Telephone: 114.54.56.78 Fax: 114.54.56.77 e-mail: caballé@wanabe.sp

BODEGAS CABALLE
Application Exercises

DIRECTIONS FOR EXERCISE 2

The following vocabulary words describe certain personality traits. Study the list and discuss which ones are suitable for characterizing the applicant you are seeking. Which ones are missing? Ask your teacher for help in expressing the qualities you are looking for.

Aggressive	Flexible
Articulate	Forgiving
Appreciative	Frank
Assertive	Friendly/Nice
Cautious	Generous
Cheerful	Open-minded
Compassionate	Optimistic
Considerate	Outgoing
Cooperative	Patient
Goal Oriented	Persistent
Honest	Practical
Insightful	Punctual
Loyal	Real/not phony
Curious/Inquisitive	Reliable
Decisive	Responsible
Discreet	Resourceful
Easy-going	Risk Taking
Effective Under Stress	Self-confident
Efficient/Productive	Sincere
Emotionally Stable	Of Sound Judgment
Energetic	Thorough
Enthusiastic	

BODEGAS CABALLE
Application Exercises

DIRECTIONS FOR EXERCISE 3

The following examples of skills may help you think about the ways of expressing the qualities in the applicant you are seeking. Study the list and find which ones are suitable for characterizing the applicant you are seeking. However, many of the ones you need may not be listed.

Listening intently	Prioritizing
Communicating warmth	Implementing new programs
Being tactful	Developing an effective team
Training people at work	Salesmanship
Assessing customers' needs	Closing a deal
Establishing rapport	Thinking quickly on your feet
Causing change	Using humor
Dealing with crisis situations	Recognizing patterns in numbers
Recognizing windows of opportunity	Working out a budget
Seeing the big picture	Scheduling
Cutting through red tape	Conceiving and generating ideas
Anticipating problems	Determining root causes
Seizing opportunities	Analyzing trends
	Acting on hunches

BODEGAS CABALLE
Application Exercises

DIRECTIONS FOR EXERCISE 4

Read the following phrases drawn from the job offers section of international newspapers for examples of how to word certain recruitment criteria in a job offer

A An acknowledged high achiever in your prime with proven success in ...

B If you are aiming for a long term career with excellent promotion prospects ...

C You will have already built up the skills and credibility to deal with clients at the highest levels.

D Do you believe you have the commitment and the drive to build an exciting new career with us?

E Will you be stimulated by the demands and the benefits of a serious, results orientated compensation package?

F You will have overall responsibility for the day-to-day ...

G You will have specific operational responsibilities to ensure that goals are achieved.

H Specifically you will be involved in ...

I The position demands a Master's degree, preferably in ...

J Excellent interpersonal and communications skills are pre-requisite as is the ability to rapidly analyze and assess customer's evolving needs as well as lead and work as a team member.

K A qualification in these fields is desirable but not essential.

L Strategic vision and the capacity to translate this vision into results-oriented action is important.

M You should have a sound understanding of market methods.

N The necessary operational skills to assist marketing planners is pre-requisite. Ideally, you will have experience of working in both ...

BODEGAS CABALLE
Application Exercises

DIRECTIONS FOR EXERCISE 5

Which of the phrases on the previous page provide the answers to the questions listed below. Copy their letters in the blanks provided.

1 Which sentence(s) targets a performance-oriented individual? ______

2 Which sentence(s) suggests challenge? ______

3 Which sentence(s) allows a variety of educational backgrounds? ______

4 Which sentence(s) ties sales with pay? ______

5 Which sentence(s) suggests the applicant should be more than a salesman? ______

6 Which sentence(s) hints at future management responsibility? ______

7 Which sentence(s) calls for a stable individual with commitment to the company? ______

8 Which sentence(s) suggests non-strategic tasks? ______

9 Which sentence(s) limits the kind of background the applicant may have? ______

10 Which sentence(s) focuses on a particular job assignment? ______

11 Which sentence(s) might cover inviting customers to lunch? ______

12 Which sentence(s) specifically focuses on the need for hard work? ______

13 Which sentence(s) calls for great experience? ______

BODEGAS CABALLE
Application Exercises

DIRECTIONS FOR EXERCISE 6

Write an advertisement for the "Central European Business" newspaper. First, refer to advertisements you have collected from the English press or the examples listed on the previous page for examples of style. Answer the following questions to help you prepare your ad.

QUESTIONS

1. How do you express the fact that the company is looking for an applicant?

____

____

____

2. How do you express the kind of company without mentioning its name?

____

____

____

3. What vocabulary suggests the importance of the company?

____

____

____

4. How do you communicate the level of challenge?

____

____

____

BODEGAS CABALLE
Application Exercises

EXERCISE 6 (cont.)

5. How do you indicate a certain level of maturity without mentioning age?

____

____

6. How do you talk about pay without specifying salary levels?

____

____

7. How do you suggest the possibility of later promotion?

____

____

8. How do you tell applicants to send you the necessary information, and that it is confidential?

____

____

BODEGAS CABALLE
Application Exercises

DIRECTIONS FOR EXERCISE 7

Now write your ad in the space below. Pay attention to phrasing your ad so as to reflect the criteria you have worked out as a group.

BODEGAS CABALLE
Application Exercises

DIRECTIONS FOR EXERCISE 8

Now read the following four recruitment reports from the **Central European Consulting and Recruiting Agency**.

Unfortunately, the CECR placed its ads, interviewed applicants and shortlisted four of them without taking your team's suggestions into account. Time is pressing and *Presidente* Caballé wants the choice to be made quickly. He has asked you to rank the candidates from 1 to 4 and be ready to defend your choices before the Selection Committee.

Debate among yourselves the qualities and drawbacks of each applicant and reach a group decision on the ranking. Be ready to take the floor when the teacher calls for a plenary debate. Be ready to apply the vocabulary and expressions you have learned in complete and complex sentences. Do not be satisfied with sentences like: "he is too old" or "she is too young" which lack subtlety and persuasive power. When pointing out applicant's strengths or weaknesses, be specific and link all your ideas in one sentence. Learn to say things like:

When opposing an applicant

"We feel Mr. X lacks the necessary educational background for the job. He will not understand......"

"We are afraid Ms. Y will not stand up to the pressure of ....given her previous experience of........"

When supporting the choice of an applicant

"His/her background in ....should be readily transferable to the selling of ...."

"With his knowledge of ...., he will easily grasp buyers' problems and be able to........"

ENJOY YOUR DEBATE!

BODEGAS CABALLE
Application Exercises

RECRUITMENT REPORT ON APPLICANT
Client: Bodegas Caballé

CECR

NAME	Boleslaw Piasecki
NATIONALITY	Polish
AGE	39
ADDRESS	Warsaw, Poland
MARITAL STATUS	Single
PRESENT EMPLOYER	Torum Hotel and Restaurant Group of Central Europe since 1993. Started as a waiter.

POSITION
Catering Services and Purchasing Manager. In charge of buying all foods, wines and other supplies for the group.

REASON FOR LEAVING
Claims hotel compensation package does not reflect the margin he generates for the hotel through cost-effective buying and management control.

PROFESSIONAL BACKGROUND
Priest, taught history in Madrid.

EDUCATION
Graduated from a Polish seminary. Ph.D. in History from a Spanish University.

LANGUAGES
Polish native. Fluent Spanish. Good Italian and Russian. Some English.

SALARY EXPECTED
$65,000 and commission plus car and expenses.

FURTHER INFORMATION
Highly unusual background. Comes from an aristocratic family. Educated in a Jesuit school. Spent a period of time in a Spanish monastic order. Left the priesthood for the business world seven years ago. Employer says he has an overbearing manner and likes the «good life» too much. May disappear for short periods without explanation, but his work has not suffered. The joke runs that his private life is behind an 'iron curtain'.

INTERVIEW ASSESSMENT
A sophisticated man. Obviously quite well read on everything. Very articulate. Expensive dress. Deep insight into market developments in Poland and Central Europe. Widely traveled throughout Europe and the World. Great knowledge of wines and growers in Europe.

BODEGAS CABALLE
Application Exercises

RECRUITMENT REPORT ON APPLICANT
Client: Bodegas Caballé

CECR

NAME	Maria de la Garriga
NATIONALITY	Spanish
AGE	32
ADDRESS	Warsaw, Poland
MARITAL STATUS	Divorced. Two children
PRESENT EMPLOYER	University of Cracow since 1997

POSITION
Coordinator of International Relations and Placement. Handles all inter-university contacts and job placement for foreign students with companies in Poland.

REASON FOR LEAVING
Finds the position too stultifying. Has long wanted to get back into sales and away from a desk job. Tired of the academic life and wants a more «hands-on» job.

PROFESSIONAL BACKGROUND
Sold wines and spirits to supermarkets and wine stores for a leading distiller/distributor in the Barcelona area to pay for her college education. Ran a business education program abroad for a leading Spanish university for the 5 years preceding her current job.

EDUCATION
Degree in Foreign Literature and Languages, University of Barcelona.

LANGUAGES
Native Spanish. Fluent Russian. Good English. Some Polish.

SALARY EXPECTED
$55,000 and commission, plus expenses.

FURTHER INFORMATION
Was originally attracted by business, but was awarded a faculty assistantship position at the Spanish university. Evolved into educational project management where she stood out for her overall planning skills. Handled executive training programs delivered by her university in Russian universities. Coordinated all faculty and finance. In time grew tired of what she regarded as a «macho» university culture in Spain.

INTERVIEW ASSESSMENT
Energetic, nervous woman with apparently great drive. Talks enthusiastically about a move into selling. Great self-assurance, bordering on conceit. Says she has developed contacts with major retailers through her placement activities.

BODEGAS CABALLE
Application Exercises

RECRUITMENT REPORT ON APPLICANT
Client: Bodegas Caballé

NAME	Sergei Nikitin
NATIONALITY	Russian
AGE	29
ADDRESS	Prague, Czech Republic
MARITAL STATUS	Single
PRESENT EMPLOYER	Prague Beer Group, distributes Czech and famous Dutch beers

POSITION
Sales Representative. In charge of major accounts among British and French retailing groups. Also sells to major pub chains.

REASON FOR LEAVING
Says he would like to move into management of the sales team but feels he has 'plateaued' with the Prague Beer Group which refuses to assign him management responsibilities.

PROFESSIONAL BACKGROUND
Previously did a stint with Boston Consulting Group in New York for two years after graduation from Business School.

EDUCATION
Graduated from Moscow University. MBA from Middle West Business School.

LANGUAGES
Russian native. Fluent American English (strong Russian accent). Good Hungarian. Decent Polish.

SALARY EXPECTED
$45,000, commission, and travel.

FURTHER INFORMATION
Apparently tried to settle in the US but it did not work out. Rumor has it that he was briefly married to an American woman. Employer says he often mentions the US and refers to it as his future home. Considered a very hard worker, but always dissatisfied and critical of company management decisions. Flaunts his American MBA and consulting background.

INTERVIEW ASSESSMENT
Very talkative man, overflowing with ideas. Seems to prefer casual clothing, no tie. Wears his hair rather long, gives the impression of a poet or artist. Obviously intelligent, but showed impatience with interview questions.

BODEGAS CABALLE
Application Exercises

RECRUITMENT REPORT ON APPLICANT
Client: Bodegas Caballé

NAME	Stanislaw Michalski
NATIONALITY	French
AGE	51
ADDRESS	Douai, France.
MARITAL STATUS	Married. Second wife. Four school-aged children.
PRESENT EMPLOYER	Intersection Hypermarkets.

POSITION
Head buyer of wines and spirits for the Intersection hypermarket chain. Deals with major international spirits distributors as well as local wine and champagne producers in France.

REASON FORLEAVING
Second wife is Polish and she wishes to return to Poland to raise her family there. 4 school-aged children. He says he is also not 'comfortable' with the cultural changes occurring since the German Meier Group took over his company.

PROFESSIONAL BACKGROUND
Started with his present employer during the take-off of mass French retailing in the late 60s. Worked his way through all aspects of merchandising, stocking and ordering until he moved into buying 15 years ago as Assistant Buyer for beers. Promoted to Head Buyer of alcoholic beverages 5 years ago.

EDUCATION
High-school leaving certificate at 16. Adult education classes in languages and marketing.

LANGUAGES
French native. Decent Polish (with strong French accent) and some English.

SALARY EXPECTED
$60,000 and commission, plus car and expenses.

FURTHER INFORMATION
Well known in the Franco-Polish community in the Northern area of France. Considered a master "networker" and the driving force behind many cultural, ethnic and public service organizations working to maintain Polish identity and raise scholarships for students of Polish background. Rumored that the Meier Group has been trying to "push him out" after their takeover of Intersection.

INTERVIEW ASSESSMENT
A lively, easy-going man who speaks willingly of his contacts with known public figures. Talks knowledgeably about the changing retailing scene in Poland. Has a simple, rather unsophisticated way of expressing himself.

BODEGAS CABALLE
Application Exercises

DIRECTIONS FOR EXERCISE 9

Write a report to Mauricio Caballé, *Presidente* of ***Bodegas Caballé*** giving your recommendation about the Sales Representative to be hired.

This is a good chance to use concise vocabulary and phrasing developed during the previous exercises. Keep your report short and to the point, but sufficiently explicit to convey a certain depth of analysis and judgment. It might be structured the following way.

Paragraph 1: Introduction, which might start with:
Ex: "*We were asked to....*"

Paragraph 2: Summary of the ideal applicant profile. Explain why certain characteristics are necessary.
Ex: "*A good background in .....is needed to enable him to quickly understand customers' real problems.*"

Paragraph 3: Introduce the applicant you support and defend your choice positively
Ex: "*Mr. X should have no trouble launching our products with his wide experience in.......*"

Paragraph 4: Introduce the runner-up and defend positively but point out the one major drawback that made him second.

Paragraph 5 & 6: Two short paragraphs pointing out the shortcomings of the last two candidates, starting with, for example:
Ex: "*Despite Mr. Z's experience of........., he falls short of our requirements in the field of ....*

Paragraph 7: Typical sentences which point out your readiness to help again and hoping that your suggestions will be useful. See your teacher for help with the 'sign-off' paragraph.

Chapter 4

The MaxiFemme Ecce Homo Merger

Case Concept and Exercises
by
Kevin Jackson

240 min.

MAXIFEMME-ECCE HOMO MERGER
Lesson Overview

LANGUAGE OBJECTIVES

To acquire and utilize vocabulary related to business mergers and acquisitions, corporate structures, and human resources.
To write a company restructuring plan and present it to an audience.
To produce written business documents related to the creation of a new company following a merger.

MANAGERIAL OBJECTIVES

To evaluate the different ways in which companies are organized.
To create an organizational structure for a newly-formed company.
To analyze the profile of two companies and reconcile their distinct philosophies in light of a corporate merger.
To create a communication plan announcing the creation of a new company.

PEDAGOGICAL NOTES

The case is designed for a business English class with a maximum of 30 students. Students should be of upper-intermediate to advanced level and have some prior knowledge of the conventions of business writing in English in order to complete the written assignments. Students receive and read the case and supporting documents before coming to session one. The case requires a minimum of three hours of class time spread over three one-hour sessions. Students are required to do an additional six to eight hours of work outside of class for the various assignments before session three. The breakdown of the sessions is as follows :

1. The case is discussed, roles are assigned, assignments are explained, discussion questions are examined, and unfamiliar vocabulary or concepts are introduced.

2. Students work in small groups on their assigned tasks.

3. Students present their restructuring plan, teacher debriefs students.

MAXIFEMME-ECCE HOMO MERGER
Lesson Overview

This case offers the instructor maximum flexibility for grouping students. The case may be dealt with as a large-group (i.e. the entire class) exercise, as a small-group (4-7 students in each group) exercise, as pairwork, or as individual work. There are a variety of assignments allowing students an opportunity for both written and oral expression.

The role of the instructor is to clearly define the assignments, and objectives of the case and to guide students thinking toward relevant issues. The instructor also moves from group to group in session two to check comprehension and to verify that English is being appropriately used. The instructor may also want to play the role of Gina Loehmann or that of the silent partner mentioned in the Case Background.

DEBRIEFING

The debriefing is management and language-oriented. Depending on the students' knowledge of business, the instructor may need to go over some of the concepts presented in the case. Students may also need to do some outside research on business concepts such as manufacturing and production, competition, human resources, cost-effectiveness, chain of command, company image, productivity, manufacturing issues, and corporate culture. The instructor has the important role of aiding the students in their research by suggesting topics and resources.

MAXIFEMME-ECCE HOMO MERGER
Case Background

MAXIFEMME *

Around 25 years ago, Gina Loehmann founded MaxiFemme, a manufacturer and retailer of clothing for full-figuredwomen. At first, Ms. Loehmann's clothing line was sold indepartment stores, but later she opened a chain of company-owned and managed stores. At present, there are 30 MaxiFemme stores, primarily in large cities in the Northeast, Midwest, and Eastern seaboard. Shortly after opening its first stores, MaxiFemme expanded its product line to include clothing and accessories for women of all sizes, from petite to full-figured.

One day ten years ago, while walking through a suburban Pittsburgh shopping mall, Ms. Loehmann was struck by the number of women shopping with their children. Sensing another opportunity, Loehmann acquired the «Kiddie Duds» children's clothing manufacturer along with its manufacturing facility in Puerto Rico within a matter of weeks. Presently, the Kiddie Duds brand is sold in both department stores and in MaxiFemme's outlet stores. MaxiFemme, headquartered in New York, has manufacturing facilities in New York, South Carolina, Mississippi, and Puerto Rico.

As MaxiFemme has grown, so has the number of senior managers who report directly to Ms. Loehmann. Furthermore, because of the way the company is organized, several middle managers also report directly to her. Ms. Loehmann finds this top-heavy structure inefficient, expensive, and difficult to manage. To complicate matters, MaxiFemme would like to expand into the men's fashion sector by acquiring Ecce Homo, a men's clothing manufacturer and retailer, thereby creating a new company. This will give Loehmann's company an entry into the men's clothing sector as well as exposure in the western US. It will also bolster its reputation as a quality manufacturer and retailer of clothing for the whole family.

In order to acquire Ecce Homo, Loehmann is offering Javier Tamayo, Ecce Homo's owner and president, shares in the new company, and an undisclosed amount of cash. The seed money for the takeover is being put up by a venture capitalist acting as a silent partner on the condition that a solid reorganization plan be introduced and that the new company take a new name to reflect its new sector of activity. Without the cash from the silent partner, the deal will fall through.

MAXIFEMME-ECCE HOMO MERGER
Case Background

ECCE HOMO

Ecce Homo was created 15 years ago as a men's clothing line specializing in fashion for younger men. It has since expanded into all areas of men's fashion including formal and casual menswear, shoes, and accessories. Its products are sold in Ecce Homo franchised stores and department stores across the country. The company has experienced steady growth, and its reputation continues to flourish.

Ecce Homo products are made in its manufacturing facilities in Bakersfield, California and Tijuana, Mexico. To lower its costs, Ecce Homo has been slowly relocating jobs from its California facility to its Mexican plant. It also uses overseas subcontractors' factories, primarily in Asia, to manufacture its goods.

The company buys its shoes from manufacturers in Italy, Spain and Brazil. It uses common carriers to ship its merchandise to its franchise outlets and department stores. President and CEO, Javier Tamayo, founder of Ecce Homo, is currently in talks with MaxiFemme about a possible buyout of Ecce Homo.

MAXIFEMME-ECCE HOMO MERGER
Case Background

MAXIFEMME *

COMPANY STRUCTURE BY DIVISIONS

	FULL-FIGURED WOMEN'S	REGULAR WOMEN'S	PETITE WOMEN'S
SENIOR MANAGEMENT			
VP Sales and Marketing	1 (150K)	1 (160K)	1 (100K)
VP Production	1 (120K)	1 (140K)	1 (100K)
VP Design	1 (120K)	1 (140K)	1 (120K)
MIDDLE MANAGEMENT			
Sales Manager	2 (70K)	1 (90K)	1 (80K)
Marketing Manager	1 (100K)	1 (100K)	1 (90K)
Production Control Manager	1 (60K)	1 (70K)	1 (60K)
LINE MANAGER			
Design	3 (60K)	5 (70K)	2 (60K)
Sales Representatives	20 (50K)	40 (50K)	15 (40K)
Market Analysts	3 (50K)	6 (60K)	2 (50K)
Production Supervisors	2 (40K)	4 (30K)	2 (30K)
SUPPORT STAFF			
Administrative Assistant	5 (20K)	7 (25K)	6 (25K)
Office Personnel	2 (40K/20K)	2 (40K/20K)	2 (40K/20K)
Production Workers	200 (25K)	300 (20K)	200 (10K)

MAXIFEMME *

DEPARTMENTS

SECTOR	MIDDLE MANAGEMENT	SUPERVISORY TECHNICAL	SUPPORT STAFF
Management Retail Outlets	3 Regional Mgrs (70K)	30 Outlet Mgrs (40K)	300 Full and Part-Time Retail Staff (15K)
Accounting/Finance	2 Financial Analysts (75K)	4 Accountants (60K)	6 Office Staff (25K)
Information Technology	1 IT Coordinator (80K)	3 IT Support Staff (40K)	10 Data Entry (25K)
Human Resources	1 HR Manager (70K)	6 HR Specialists (40K)	5 Office Staff (20K)
Purchasing	1 Purchasing Manager (80K)	10 Purchasing Agents (50K)	5 Office Staff (20K)
Logistics	1 Logistics Coordinator (80K)	10 Logistics Support Staff (30K)	40 Shipping, Receiving and Inventory Control Staff (25K)
Customer Service	1 Customer Service Manager (70K)		20 Customer Service Agents (25K)

MAXIFEMME-ECCE HOMO MERGER
Case Background

ECCE HOMO

COMPANY STRUCTURE

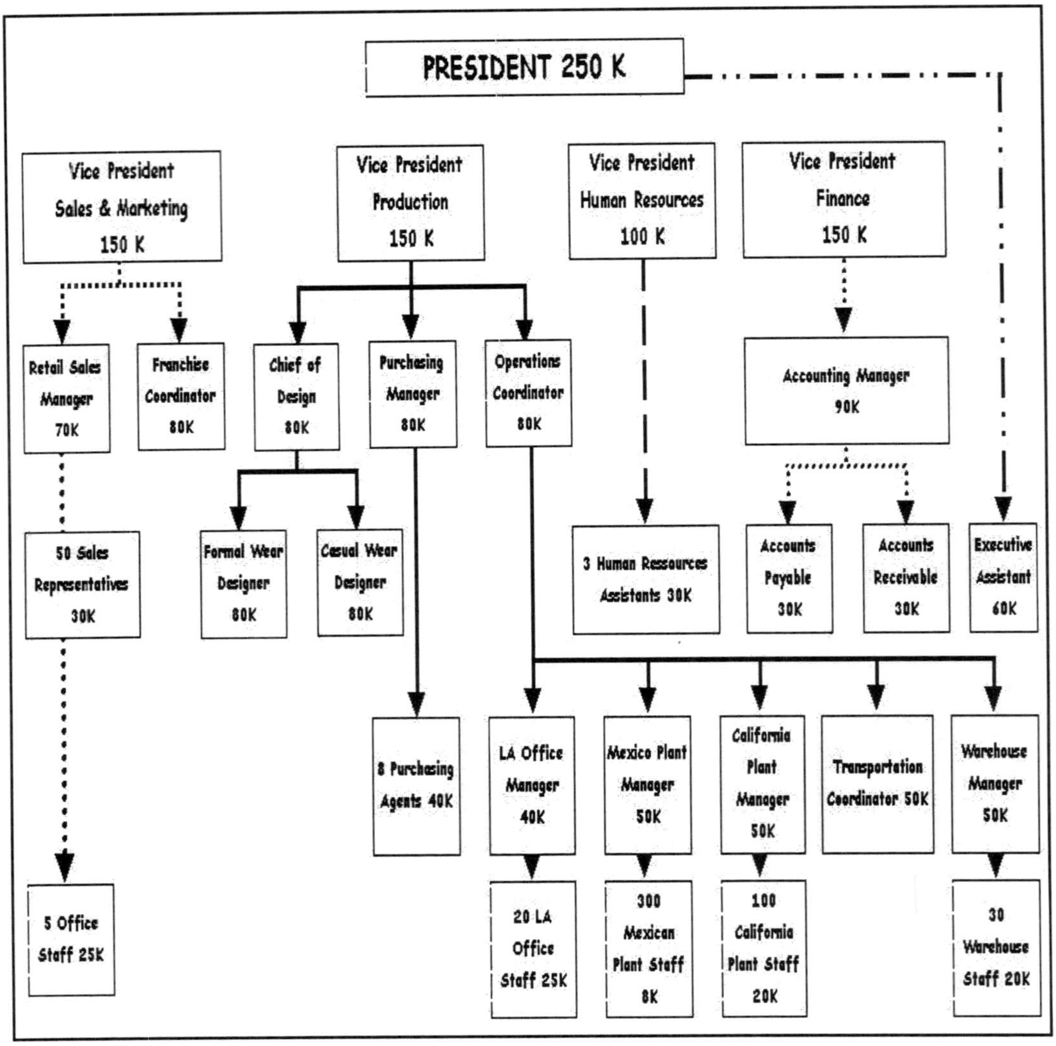

MAXIFEMME-ECCE HOMO MERGER
Case Background

MAXIFEMME *

Founded 1974 in New York
President and CEO, Gina Loehmann
Corporate Headquarters
New York, New York

Sector of Activity
Women's and children's clothing and accessories.

Distribution / Sales
Department stores, company-owned retail outlets, catalogue sales, mail order, Internet site.

Retail Outlets
Atlanta, Atlantic City, Boston, Chicago, Cleveland, Detroit, Miami, Milwaukee, Minneapolis, Myrtle Beach, Nashville, New York, Philadelphia, Pittsburgh, Washington DC

Manufacturing Facilities
Full-figured women's wear manufactured in New York. Petite women's clothing manufactured in Columbia, South Carolina.
Regular women's clothing manufactured in Pearl, Mississippi.
Children's wear manufactured in Puerto Rico.

Number of Employees
1,553

Annual Payroll
$36,820,000

Annual Sales
N/A

Company Values
Quality clothing for women and children in one store. Total company control over the product, from production to final sale. Autocratic management structure with all senior managers and some middle managers reporting directly to Ms. Loehmann. Company takes great pride that its products are «Made in USA by American workers». Fair treatment of employees, internal promotions, career opportunity, job security.

MAXIFEMME-ECCE HOMO MERGER
Case Background

ECCE HOMO

Founded 1984 in Los Angeles
President, Javier Tamayo
Corporate Headquarters, Los Angeles

Sector of Activity
Men's clothing, shoes, and accessories

Distribution / Sales
Department stores and independently-owned franchises
Franchise start-up fee is $100,000 plus cost of merchandise.

Retail Outlets
Los Angeles, San Diego, San Francisco, Sacramento, Portland, Seattle, Denver, Santa Fe, Dallas, Houston, Minneapolis, Chicago, New York, Boston, Miami, Atlanta, Las Vegas

Manufacturing Facilities
Factories in Bakersfield, California and Tijuana, Mexico.
Warehouse in Bakersfield.

Number of Employees
504

Annual Payroll
$9,215,000

Annual Sales
$100 million

Company Values

Quality men's clothing at affordable prices. Rapid expansion with a chain of independently-owned franchises. Relaxed Corporate atmosphere. Top executives have an «open door» policy. Use of manufacturing subcontractors and Mexican facilities to keep costs down has led to layoffs in recent years.

MAXIFEMME-ECCE HOMO MERGER
Application Exercises

DIRECTIONS FOR EXERCISE 1

Read the following descriptions of types of departmentalization and provide your own examples for each.

TYPES OF ORGANIZATIONAL STRUCTURE

When a company is created, it must be organized into manageable units. These units often called departments, are also known as divisions, branches, sections, bureaus or groups. These departments may be based on any one or combination of the following :

Product - based on the product(s) being sold.
Example : a store which sells consumer electronics and appliances may have departments such as the television department, stereo department, small appliances department, or large appliances department.
Your example:____

Customer - based on the specific profile of targeted customer.
Example : a bank which has consumer banking and commercial banking units or a department store which has a women's section, a men's section, and a children's section.
Your example:____

Process - based on the process used to make the product.
Example : a food manufacturer which sells dairy-based products may have a milk product department, a cheese product department, a yogurt department, or an ice cream department.
Your example:____

Geographic Zone - based on the geographic area in which the customer is located or in which the business operates.
Example : A company which is organized along regional lines : In the US, this might consist of a Northeast region, a Southern region, a Midwest region, and a Western region.
Your example:____

Function - based on the group's principal activity.
Example : A firm which has production, finance, human resources, customer service, and information technology departments.
Your example:____

MAXIFEMME-ECCE HOMO MERGER
Application Exercises

DIRECTIONS FOR EXERCISE 3

Go back and read about MaxiFemme and Ecce Homo and look at their company structure charts and decide which type(s) of departmentalization each uses.

DIRECTIONS FOR EXERCISE 4

The following questions may be used as a guide to help students focus their thoughts about the merger. The questions are relevant to one or more of the following areas:

(PO) Production and Operations
(HRM) Human Resources and Management
(MPR) Media and Public Relations
(RD) Retail and Distribution

1. What are some of the advantages and drawbacks of subcontracting production? (PO, HRM)
2. What type of departmentalization will work best? Why? (PO, HRM,)
3. What should the image of the new company be? (MPR)
4. Who are the targeted clients of the new company? (MPR, RD)
5. What type of damage control measures will be instituted to protect the reputation of the new company in light of imminent layoffs? (MPR, HRM)
6. Which stores, if any, should be closed? (HRM, RD)
7. What should be done about the franchises? (RD, HRM)
8. Where should new stores be opened? (RD)
9. Which other clothing manufacturers have opened retail clothing outlets? (RD)
10. Where should the new company have its headquarters? (PO, HRM, MPR, RD)

MAXIFEMME-ECCE HOMO MERGER
Application Exercises

11. What type of separation package will be offered to downsized employees? (HRM)

12. Make a list of specific articles / services sold by MaxiFemme and Ecce Homo. What other products could be offered in the future? (RD, PO)

13. Which people work at the headquarters of each company? (HRM)

14. What type of jobs do each of the following do? (HRM, PO)

- Executive Assistant	- Office Staff
- Human Resources Manager	- Human Resources Assistant
- Production Control Manager	- Customer Service
- Warehouse Staff	- Accounts Payable Clerk
- Accounts Receivable Clerk	- Transportation Coordinator

15. What are some of the possible reasons for the salary disparities at MaxiFemme? (HRM, PO)

16. Decide on a new name for the company to reflect its new image. (MPR, HRM, PO, RD)

17. Which middle managers report directly to Ms. Loehmann? (HRM)

DIRECTIONS FOR EXERCISE 5

The following vocabulary either appears in the MaxiFemme - Ecce Homo case or may be useful to students in preparing their presentations or written work. Students should familiarize themselves with the terms. If possible, some class time should be set aside for discussion.

acquisition	chain of command	common carrier	franchise
to downsize	to streamline	human resources	layoff (to)
subcontractor	merger	takeover	manufacturing
outplacement	severance pay	open door policy	retail
silent partner	customer service	to put up (money)	trend
retail	to fall through	mission statement	to report to
seed money	undisclosed	job security	top-heavy

MAXIFEMME-ECCE HOMO MERGER
Application Exercises

OPTION 1 - Large Group Work

The class is divided into four groups of equal numbers. Each group works on a specific aspect of the restructuring. This work is begun in session two and finished as homework for session three. As the different groups are all «working» for the same consulting company, it is of utmost importance that the groups communicate with one another. The class presents its conclusions and recommendations as a cohesive unit. The groups work on the following areas :

Production and Operations

This group is responsible for determining the production policy of the new company. Its chief aim is to decide how and where production is to be carried out. The group makes recommendations on how many production workers are needed in the new company and where production facilities are to be located. It also gives an indication as to the number of layoffs anticipated and the savings to the company. Students may want to research labor costs and practices - both inside and outside the USA, subcontracting possibilities - both domestic and abroad, import and customs restrictions, and methods of tranportation.

Human Resources and Management

This group makes recommendations about the restructuring of the work force and the overall organization of the new company. This group also ultimately decides on the number of employees adversely affected by the formation of the new company, and proposes a termination policy, including a compensation scheme, for those employees losing their jobs. It is also in charge of communicating this information, in writing or verbally, to management and the employees. Finally, the group is also responsible for proposing a human resources policy for the new company (i.e. vacations, sick pay, promotion policy, evaluations, etc.) Students may want to research labor laws and practices in the US, the outplacement industry, and severance pay practices.

Media and Public Relations

This group is responsible for creating and launching the media campaign and for suggesting a name and logo for the new company. It recommends types of media to be used to give maximum exposure to the new company. This group will also create advertisements using print, audio or video as a medium. Students may want to research other companies who have changed their names and images and the effects, both negative and positive, as well as recent mergers and acquisitions.

Retail and Distribution

This group is responsible for establishing a retail policy for the new company. This includes recommending which stores are to remain open, which are to be closed, and where new stores should be opened, as well as the physical layout of the stores. This group also needs to consider what to do with the independently owned Ecce Homo franchises scattered around the country. Finally, the retail group will want to consider what new product lines can and should be added to the present collections. Students may want to research the retail clothing sector, demographic trends in the US, franchising, and on-line retailing.

MAXIFEMME-ECCE HOMO MERGER
Application Exercises

DIRECTIONS FOR EXERCISE 6

Many companies use a combination of some or all of the forms of departmentalization. For example, a company's top-level may be functionally departmentalized, with its sales force being departmentalized along geographical lines, and a production department which is organized around a process of customer profile.

Look at the following organizational chart of a staple and nail manufacturer and try to determine the type (s) of departmentalization being used.

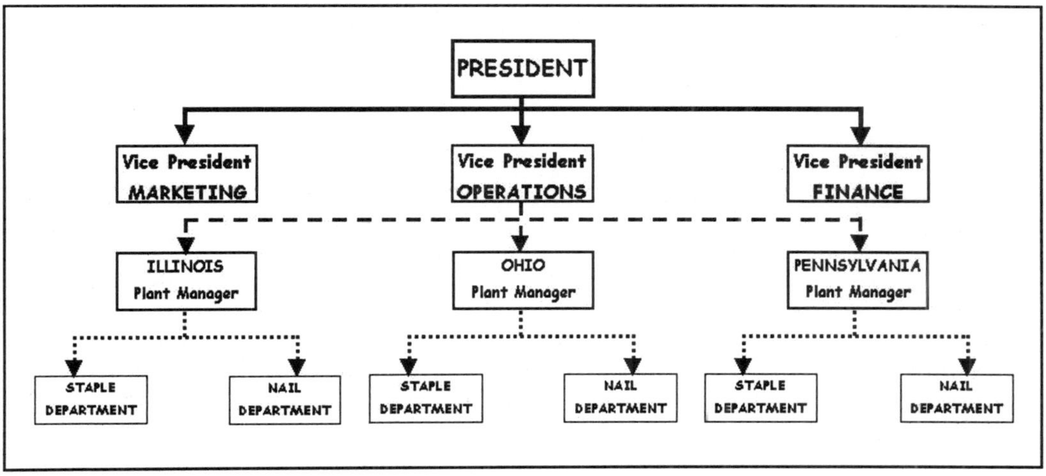

MAXIFEMME-ECCE HOMO MERGER
Application Exercises

DIRECTIONS FOR EXERCISE 7

Your consulting company has won a very lucrative contract from Gina Loehmann to provide a reorganization plan for her new company following the MaxiFemme-Ecce Homo merger. Using the information on the previous pages and information which you gather from outside research :

1. Decide on an organizational structure for Ms. Loehmann's new company
2. Develop an organizational chart for the company indicating the chain of command.
3. Indicate which departments are to be merged, if any, and which operations are to be discontinued.
4. Indicate any new departments or operations to be put into place.
5. Indicate the number of jobs to be cut and approximate savings to the company in salaries
6. Determine what compensation, if any, will be given to terminated employees.
7. Write a new philosophy or mission statement for the new company
8. Choose a new name for the company
9. Develop a publicity campaign for the new company
10. Anticipate who will support your proposals and who will oppose them.

When making your decisions, consider the different types of departmentalization that companies use. You may want to research labor practices and costs to help you determine a policy toward layoffs and production. You may also want to consider other possibilities such as sub-contracting (either domestically or abroad), job-sharing, or department combining. Be prepared to present your plan at the next class session using graphics where appropriate.

OPTION 2 - Small Group Work

Form groups of four students each. Each group presents its reorganization plan with one student working in each of the areas of Production and Operations, Human Resources and Management, Media and Public Relations, and Retail and Distribution.

OPTION 3 - Individual Work

Individual students are responsible for drawing up their own reorganization plans following the guidelines laid out in the Large Group Work section above. Their findings and conclusions can then either be presented orally or in a formal written report.

MAXIFEMME-ECCE HOMO MERGER
Application Exercises

RELATED ASSIGNMENTS

1. You are the head of the consulting team which has been hired by Gina Loehmann to propose a restructuring plan for her new company. Draft a letter to her giving a general overview of your conclusions.

2. As head of Human Resources, draft a memo to employees in which you notify them of their termination from the company as a result of restructuring. Be sure to include that the Human Resources Department will be seeing each individual employee to discuss the terms of separation.

3. You work for the Public Relations Department of the company. Write a press release in which you announce the merger between MaxiFemme and Ecce Homo.

4. You are a journalist. Write a newspaper article or present a TV or radio news announcement in which you discuss the merger between MaxiFemme and Ecce Homo.

5. Create a print, radio, or television advertisement for the newly formed company.

6. You have recently been hired to create an Internet web site for Ms. Loehmann's new company. Draft a letter to Ms. Loehmann offering suggestions of what you think ought to be included on the site.

7. Write the mission statement for the new company.

8. Create a promotional brochure to be distributed in the cities where the company stores are located.

BIBLIOGRAPHY

Daft, R., *Organizational Theory and Design*, 4th edition. St.Paul, MN : West Publishing, 1992.

Griffin, R.W. and Ebert, R.J.. *Business*, 3rd edition. Englewood Cliffs, NJ : Prentice Hall, 1993.

Chapter 5

Van Haffner Toys

Case Concept by

Stephanie and Marcus Hurt

Exercises by

Christine Coisne

180 min.

VAN HAFFNER TOYS
Lesson Overview

LANGUAGE OBJECTIVES

Acquiring key accounting terms
Identifying differences between American and British terminology
Developing language skills by exchanging technical information
Defending one's point of view in dealing with technical data
Style switching and report writing

MANAGERIAL OBJECTIVES

Introducing financial statements
Analyzing financial data

PEDAGOGICAL NOTES

The students should be able to analyze financial statements in their native language.

This unit requires students to use accounting vocabulary in a practical context. It introduces the main financial statements needed to describe and analyze company performance.

Groups of 20 to 30 students are perfectly suited for this exercise. Small group work alternates with plenary sessions. Written work may be done individually or in teams, as an in-class exercise or at home.

Through highly interactive exercises, students communicate and analyse credible information contained in accounting documents.

The teacher should move from group to group, helping with vocabulary acquisition and pointing out the most common mistakes and communication problems to use during the debriefing sessions. In the plenary sessions, the teacher should play the role of a facilitator assisting the students in explaining findings and their line of reasoning.

VAN HAFFNER TOYS
Lesson Overview

PREPARATION AND CLASS PLAN

The in-class work can be divided into the following stages :

1. **Converting American accounting documents into British format**

   In groups of four or five students, students convert the company's financial statements into British style and describe similarities and differences. During this phase the teacher should work with each group successively to help them determine differences in vocabulary and check application exercises: *45 minutes.*

2. **Describing and analyzing financial statements**

   Working in small groups, students describe and analyze financial data. Using general accounting principles, they inventory the company's main weaknesses. Once they have done this, the groups must be ready to compare and defend their findings orally in plenary session: *45 minutes.*

3. **Board meeting and report writing**

   Students make a list of possible recommendations to Van Haffner. For this purpose, small groups of students simulate a Board meeting, thereby interpreting their financial analysis into ways of improving the current situation. After a close examination of corporate banking services, they devise a suitable financing package. A brief report is then drafted to allow students to convert oral exchanges into writing. At this stage, the teacher should work with each group to help them word their recommendations in the most appropriate way: *45 minutes.*

4. **Debating alternatives**

   In plenary session, the teacher writes the solutions put forward by each group on a flipchart. Debate should be encouraged and students should be able to defend their viewpoint. At the end of the debate, groups will have agreed on a sound proposal. As a wrap-up exercise, students may be asked to simulate the meeting between Van Haffner and the Chief Lending Officer: *45 minutes.*

VAN HAFFNER TOYS
Case Background

Paul Van Haffner, CEO of Van Haffner Toy Co., Antwerpt, the Netherlands, called on the Chief Commercial Lending Officer of the newly established Nikko Bank in Leicester, to seek financing for an expansion plan he had been working on. He was planning to set up operations in the U.K. and wanted Nikko to help fund his venture. After an hour of conversation, Van Haffner left the Bank the basic financial statements of his corporation and agreed to meet with the Officer in two weeks during his next visit to the U.K. to scout for distributors for his products.

YOUR ASSIGNMENT

You are a student from a leading Graduate School of Management performing a traineeship at the Nikko Bank assigned to assisting the Chief Commercial Lender. He has asked you to prepare a report on Van Haffner Toys and turn it in to him in time for the meeting with Van Haffner. He has left you with the notes he took during the appointment with the CEO as well as the financial statements of the company.

You are to convert the American-style reports into British style. He also expects you to provide clear insight into the creditworthiness of the company as well as soundly argued suggestions on a suitable financing package. He counts your background in financial analysis for a thorough understanding of the company's problem areas.

THE BANK OFFICER'S NOTES

Van Haffner seems like a rough and ready risk-taker. He's pretty sure of himself. He built his business from scratch and has turned it into one of the leading innovative toy companies in Northern Europe. This has been done without going public, calling occasionally on American financial partners and continental European banks. Intending to go transnational, he is looking for opportunities in the U.K., attractive, as he says, both for its potential toy sales and its entrepreneurial approach to lending.

The company has recorded an unusually high growth rate for such a seasonal business in a highly competitive industry. Recent changes in the toy business have made it necessary to refurbish the company's plant, and Van Haffner has sold off some of the older assets in order to buy in new equipment to retool his line. He seems very bent on fast growth in sales volume and beefing up market share, but seems a bit flippant when it comes to ROI. He made light of my comments on his declining profitability. He also asked me what I thought about a possible IPO on the British market in a few years.

VAN HAFFNER TOYS
Case Background

INCOME STATEMENT FOR THE FISCAL YEARS ENDING December 31, 1996-1999 (in thousands of Euros)

	1996	1997	1998	1999
Net sales	21 290	27 677	35 980	46 774
Cost of goods sold	16 240	20 625	26 193	33 266
Gross Profit	5 050	7 052	9 787	13 508
Selling and Administrative Expenses	3 260	4 401	6 602	10 677
Depreciation	390	507	659	857
Interest Expense	270	540	1 080	2 160
Other expense (income)	- 80	- 104	- 135	-176
Profit before tax	1 210	1 708	1 581	- 10
Tax	590	850	540	0
Extraordinary Charges	210	0	0	500
Net Income	410	858	1 041	- 510

BALANCE SHEETS FOR THE FISCAL YEARS ENDING December 31, 1996-1999 (in thousands of Euros)

ASSETS	1996	1997	1998	1999
Cash	90	30	124	10
Marketable Securities	150	250	350	115
Accounts receivable	2 070	2 858	4 312	8 277
Inventory (LIFO)	4 570	5 941	7 723	10 040
Prepaid Expenses	120	150	150	200
Current assets	7 000	9 079	12 659	18 642
Net fixed assets	1 970	2 561	3 329	3 628
Other assets	280	284	430	215
Total Assets	9 250	11 924	16 419	22 485
LIABILITIES AND OWNERS' EQUITY				
Notes payable	2 940	1 236	3 636	9 740
Accounts payable - trade	2 900	3 770	4 524	5 655
Corporate taxes payable	90	40	640	270
Current maturity long-term debt	130	100	340	390
Accruals	460	460	250	320
Current liabilities	6 520	5 606	9 390	16 375
Deferred taxes	100	100	120	120
Long-term debt	90	2 820	2 470	2 060
Total liabilities	6 710	8 526	11 980	18 555
Common stock/retained earnings	80	80	80	80
Retained earnings	2 460	3 318	4 359	3 850
Total owners' equity	2 540	3 398	4 439	3 930
Total liabilities/owners' equity	9 250	11 924	16 419	22 485

VAN HAFFNER TOYS
Application Exercises

DIRECTIONS FOR EXERCISE 1

Look into the financial statements provided by Van Haffner and convert the American balance sheets and income statements into British style using the following samples which illustrate conversion examples. Beforehand, do vocabulary exercises on pages 4 and 5 to help you carry out the conversion.

American balance sheet (in Euros)

Assets	
Cash	100
Marketable Securities	200
Accounts receivable	1 400
Prepaid expenses	200
Inventory	2 100
Current assets	4 000
Net fixed assets	5 000
Other assets	1 000
Total assets	10 000
Liabilities & Stockholders'equity	
Notes payable	1 000
Accounts payable-trade	500
Corporate taxes payable	200
Current maturity long-term debt	100
Accruals	200
Current liabilities	2 000
Deferred taxes	200
Long-term debt	800
Stockholders'equity	
Common stock	6 000
Retained earnings	1 000
Total liabilities and **Owners' equity**	10 000

British balance sheet (in Euros)

Assets	
Fixed assets	5 000
Investment	1 000
	6 000
Current assets	
Stocks	2 100
Debtors	1 400
Quoted investments	200
Prepaid expenses	200
Cash	100
less Current Liabilities	
Trade Creditors	500
Bills payable	1 000
Corporation tax	200
Short-term loan	100
Accrued expenses	200
Net working capital	**2 000**
Net worth	
Share capital	6 000
Reserves	1 000
Long-term liabilities	
Long-term loans	1 000
TOTAL	**8 000**

American income statement

Revenues (net sales)	40 000
Less cost of goods sold	30 000
Gross profit	10 000
Selling and administrative expenses	2 500
Depreciation	400
Interest expense	100
= ***Income before taxes***	7 000
less tax	3 500
Extraordinary charges	1 000
= ***Net income***	2 500

British profit and loss account

Turnover	40 000
Less cost of sales	30 000
Gross profit	10 000
Selling and administrative expenses	2 500
Gross operating profit	7 500
Depreciation	400
Interest expense	100
= ***Net operating profit***	7 000
less corporation tax	3 500
Extraordinary expenses	1 000
= ***Net profit after tax***	2 500

VAN HAFFNER TOYS
Application Exercises

DIRECTIONS FOR EXERCISE 2

Fill in the following table using the sample financial statements to help you identify differences in terminology.

AMERICAN ENGLISH	BRITISH ENGLISH	DEFINITION	EXAMPLE
Accounts payable	1. Creditors	Money owed to creditors	Bank Overdraft
2. Accounts Receivable	Debtors	Money owed by debtors	5000 Euros for the sale of 250 dolls
Common stock	3. Share Capital	The total value of shares issued by a company	20 shares valued at 4 Euros each
Fiscal year	Financial year	4.	03.31.98/03.31.99
5. Net Income	Net profit after tax	The balance of profit and loss account after all expenses have been paid	___ Euros in 1999
Income statement	6. Profit & Loss (P+L)	The history book of the company	In the 1996 income statement, net income stands at 410,000 euros
7.	8.	The value of total stocks	Raw materials, work in progress and finished goods
Notes	9.	Commercial paper	Promissory notes
Stockholders' equity	10. Net worth	Shares plus reserves	___ Euros in 1999
Marketable securities	11.	Short-term securities that can be traded on the stock market	Treasury bonds
12.	Accrued Expenses	Business expenses incurred during a financial year that have not been paid yet	Taxes on salaries and wages

VAN HAFFNER TOYS
Application Exercises

DIRECTIONS FOR EXERCISE 3

Some key accounting words are used in both British and American English.

1. Match the definitions and examples with the following words in order to finalize your conversion.

Depreciation	Net working capital	Current assets
Corporation Tax	Long-term debt	Fixed Assets
Retained Earnings	Current liabilities	

ITEM	DEFINITION	EXAMPLE	SELF-TEST
1	That part of net income that is not distributed to shareholders.	100,000 Euros were reinvested in the business last year.	
2	Assets that can be quickly converted into cash.	This customer has not paid off his debt.	
3	The tax on profits made by companies.	The current rate is 28%.	
4	Nonliquid Assets such as land, buildings and machinery or licenses and registered trademarks.	The plant has been upgraded and a new administrative building has been built.	
5	Debts to be paid within one year of the date of the financial statement.	Suppliers are paid 90 days after delivery.	
6	The conversion of the value of a fixed asset into an expense to enable the company to replace that asset.	We will write down 20% of the total value of the machine each year for 5 years.	
7	Current assets minus current liabilities.	We will need to generate more cash to compensate for the cost overruns.	
8	The capital borrowed by a business in order to provide for its long-term finance.	We will have to issue debentures in order to finance our expansion plan.	

VAN HAFFNER TOYS
Application Exercises

DIRECTIONS FOR EXERCISE 3 (cont.)

Match the following items with the the self test area in exercise 3.

A- Some business expenses such as donations to charities are tax deductible
B- The new automated machine will be written off over a ten-year period
C- We have £ 30,000 on our current account right now
D- The bank will not renew the authorized overdraft
E- Intangible assets include patents, licences and registered trademarks
F- Working capital will not be sufficient to cover the overheads
G- £ 500,000 were ploughed back in the business last year
H- The loan taken out in 1996 will have to be paid back by 2006, principal and interest

DIRECTIONS FOR EXERCISE 4

Working in groups, explain the difference between a profit and loss account and a balance sheet by answering the following questions :

1. What kind of financial information is recorded in Van Haffner's profit and loss account?

___

___

2. What kind of financial information appears on Van Haffner's balance sheet?

___

___

3. What key financial data enable a financial manager to monitor short-term solvency and long-term solvency?

___

___

4. How does a financial manager measure a company's profitability?

___

___

5. How can a company's creditworthiness be assessed?

___

___

VAN HAFFNER TOYS
Application Exercises

DIRECTIONS FOR EXERCISE 5

By examining the following summary, describe the major trends that have affected the company's finance in the 4 years under review.

PROFIT AND LOSS ACCOUNT
(in rounded figures)

ITEM	1996	1997	1998	1999
Turnover	21 300	27 700	36 000	46 800
Cost of goods sold	16 200	20 700	26 200	33 300
Gross profit	5 100	7 000	9 800	13 500
Selling and administrative expenses	3 300	4 400	6 600	10 700
Gross operating profit	1 800	2 600	3 200	2 800
Other expenses	600	900	1 600	2 900
Net operating profit	1 200	1 700	1 600	-10
Tax	600	900	600	0
Extraordinary expenses	200	0	0	500
Net profit after tax	400	800	1 000	- 510

BALANCE SHEET
(in rounded figures)

ITEM	1996	1997	1998	1999
Total fixed assets	2 300	2 900	3 800	3 900
Current assets	7 000	9 100	13 000	18 600
Current liabilities	6 500	5 600	9 400	16 400
Net working capital	500	3 500	3 300	2 300
Net Worth	2 540	3 400	4 450	3 850
Long-term liabilities	200	2 900	2 600	2 200

VAN HAFFNER TOYS
Application Exercises

DIRECTIONS FOR EXERCISE 6

Identify the main financial weaknesses of Van Haffner Toy Co and present your findings to another group. Discuss similarities and differences. Be ready to take the floor when the teacher calls for a plenary debate. Before doing so, make sure you can answer the following questions:

1. SHORT-TERM FINANCE

a. How can the increase in current assets be explained?

____

____

b. How can the increase in current liabilities be interpreted?

____

____

2. LONG-TERM FINANCE

a. Is the firm able to meet its long-term liabilities?

____

____

b. What do you think of the adequacy of the capital structure?

____

____

3. PROFITABILITY

a. Why did the company register a net loss in 1999?

____

____

b. What are the expenses growing faster than revenues?

____

____

VAN HAFFNER TOYS
Application Exercises

DIRECTIONS FOR EXERCISE 7

Groups of 4 now simulate a Board meeting to interpret the previous analysis and determine which financial flows need improvement. They answer the following questions :

1. Is the stock valuation method (LIFO) the right one ?
2. How can the company make sales more cost-effective ?
3. What about a cost accounting system ?
4. Should Van Haffner raise venture capital ?

Production Manager	Thanks to streamlining and innovation, the factory is turning out more and more products. However, stock level is up.	
Sales Manager	The sales team has been reorganised : sales results have exceeded forecasts by 25% in the last 2 years. Sales commissions have followed suit.	
Finance Manager	In spite of the successive warnings sent out to production and sales, the financial situation is deteriorating. Profitability is down.	
CEO	The company is now ready to find new outlets for its products and set up operations in the UK. NIKKO will surely back up an expansion plan.	

VAN HAFFNER TOYS
Application Exercises

DIRECTIONS FOR EXERCISE 8

The following memo has been left on your desk together with the toys market sales forecasts as a support for your assignment. These documents are meant to help you devise a suitable financing package.

MEMORANDUM

From : Chief Lending Officer
To : All trainees
Date : April 30, 1999
Subject : Update on bank policy

Short-term financial services

Authorizing an overdraft facility
- Maximum amount : 4 000 Euros
- Interest charged : 5%

Discounting bills of exchange
- Bank charges : 4%

Extending a line of credit
- Interest charged : 4.5%

Selling quoted investments
- No commission

Long-term financial services

Granting a long-term, secured loan
- Assets serve as a collateral
- Interest charged : 4.20 %

Granting a long-term, unsecured loan
- Interest charged : 6.20 %

Underwriting issue of shares
- Bank fees : 1 %

Selling leasing packages
- Bank charges : 3% of purchasing price

VAN HAFFNER TOYS
Application Exercises

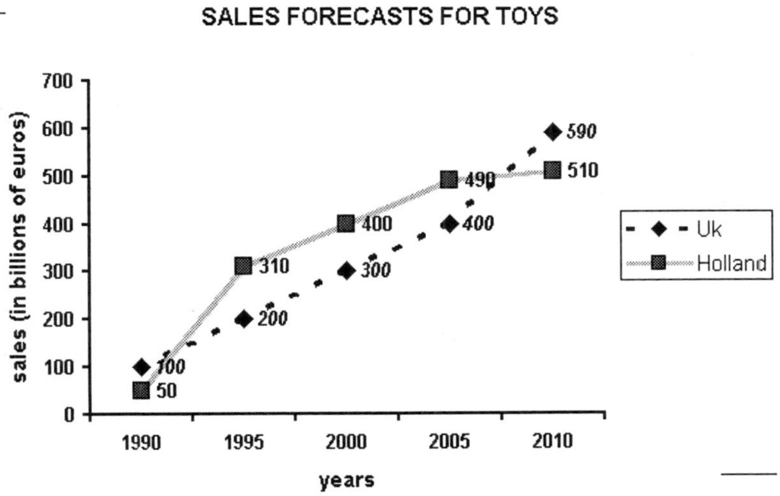

Sales (in billions of Euros)
(Source : Kwan Marketing Association)

DIRECTIONS FOR EXERCISE 9

Discuss the possible alternatives by answering some questions:

1. How can Van Haffner bring interest payment down?

____

____

2. What are the advantages and drawbacks of a secured loan?

____

____

3. Should the company have its bills discounted?

____

____

4. To what extent can Van Haffner consider an Initial Public Offering?

____

____

VAN HAFFNER TOYS
Application Exercises

DIRECTIONS FOR EXERCISE 10

Write a short, accurate report to the Chief Lending Officer. Read the following phrases drawn from previous financial statement analyses. Use the words and phrases in italics to draft your version.

Findings

A- *Although* net sales have slightly increased *compared to*

____

B- Net income has recorded a considerable drop *in spite of*

____

C- Selling and administrative expenses have more than quadrupled in the years under review *whereas*

____

D- *Similarly* increased interest expense has contributed to declining profitability

____

E- *In contrast to* ………………… the company is not able to generate sufficient cash flow

____

Recommendations

A- The company *should* monitor ______________________________

B- Customers *may* be willing to ______________________________

C- Creditors *might* object to ______________________________

D- Net working capital *could* be improved if ______________________________

E- Current liabilities *will have to be* ______________________________

VAN HAFFNER TOYS
Application Exercises

From: **Date:**
To: **Subject:**

Introduction: Summary of assignment

Findings
Review of income statements

Review of balance-sheets

Recommendations

VAN HAFFNER TOYS
Application Exercises

DIRECTIONS FOR EXERCISE 11

Role-play: The Chief Lending Officer meets with Van Haffner.

The Officer has congratulated you on the excellent report you have written. He is not ready to start any business with Van Haffner if the company does not accept what the bank has to offer.

Role A: The Chief Lending Officer points out the financial weaknesses of the company and presents the package.

Role B: Van Haffner is eager to break into the British market and is ready for sound advice.

BIBLIOGRAPHY

Mackenzie, I., *Financial English*, Language Teaching Publications, 1995.

Van der Yeught, Michel., *Anglais comptable et comptabilité anglo-saxonne*, Ellipses, 1992.

Weston, J.F. and Copeland, T., *Managerial Finance*, Cassell Educational Limited, 1988.

Chapter 6

McCarthy's Nickel and Dime Store

Case Concept and Exercises
by
Anne E. Witte

360 min.

McCARTHY'S NICKEL AND DIME STORE
Lesson Overview

LANGUAGE OBJECTIVES

To acquire and to utilize the vocabulary related to the retail trade
To analyze technical information and draw conclusions from charts, tables and spread sheets
To write a report based on this case exercising strategic thinking

MANAGERIAL OBJECTIVES

To consider options for enhancing profit in the retail trade
To interpret financial documents
To weigh different strategies and choose the most feasible one
To forecast market trends

PEDAGOGICAL NOTES

The case is read in class and the language and managerial objectives are carefully explained to the students. The application exercises can be run immediately thereafter, or corrected after homework preparation. The class is then broken down into task forces of four persons. The prepare their analysis of the case. The oral presentations should last 15 minutes and be presented in the presence of other students. The case debriefing is conducted in class with the full group. During the presentations, students chosen at random react to the reports by asking questions and challenging decisions.

DEBRIEFING

The debriefing should be both marketing and language oriented. The content debriefing may require exchanging information with marketing professionals in order to offer a comparative insight on the subject. For the environmental information, students will need to integrate supermarket and demographical trends in their conclusions. The teacher should concentrate on reviewing with students what information is important for a three year projection and what information can be put aside temporarily. A vocabulary quiz is useful to double-check that technical and financial vocabulary has been integrated.

McCARTHY'S NICKEL AND DIME STORE
Case Background

McCarthy's Nickel and Dime Store was first opened in 1947 in Deerwater, Kansas. Initially a Mom and Pop candy store and soda fountain run by the McCarthy family, it grew into a general store in the 1950's supplying the neighborhood with sundry items including textiles, plastics, cleaning fluids, pet food, greeting cards, packaged food and seasonal specials.

The store has become a local legend and generations of local families have enjoyed the ice-cream and soda legacy that McCarthy's has so well maintained. Patrons take pleasure in crossing the original floorboards which have been maintained and selecting candy from the old wooden drawers in which it has always been stored. The sign outside is the original metal engraving in old-fashioned, hand-crafted lettering. The wooden steps leading up to two creaky screen doors open into one main room with a high ceiling. A soda fountain and stools are located on the left while two cashiers saddle the front doors. The merchandise is displayed along aisles of neatly arranged shelves. The stock is kept in the basement.

The McCarthy family holds a position of status in Deerwater. The small business passed into the hands of the sons and daughters of the McCarthy's in the 1960's and the eldest grandchild is now preparing for taking over the concern by preparing a degree in business administration. In all, seven people are employed full-time at McCarthy's.

Although the store did well in the 1960's and 1970's, profits have been decreasing slowly but consistently since the mid 80's. Clearly, local competition has been partly the cause for this. Giant supermarkets located in supermalls just outside the town, with free parking, regular sales and a series of coupon offers attract most of the middle-class, money-saving families. However, McCarthy's still corresponds to the needs of a different type of clientele content with paying a little more for the convenience of a nearby general supplies store which still provides personalized service.

McCarthy's Nickel and Dime Store
Case Background

It has now become necessary to more aggressively define the specificity of the general store to ensure future profit. Around the dinner table, the children and grandchildren agreed on the key points which needed greater attention:

overall store strategy
store's renovation
merchandising
pricing policy
buying policy

They then assembled all the information they could find about the business. Below, are the original architectural plans of the ground floor. It has remained the same since the store's opening.

STORE LAYOUT

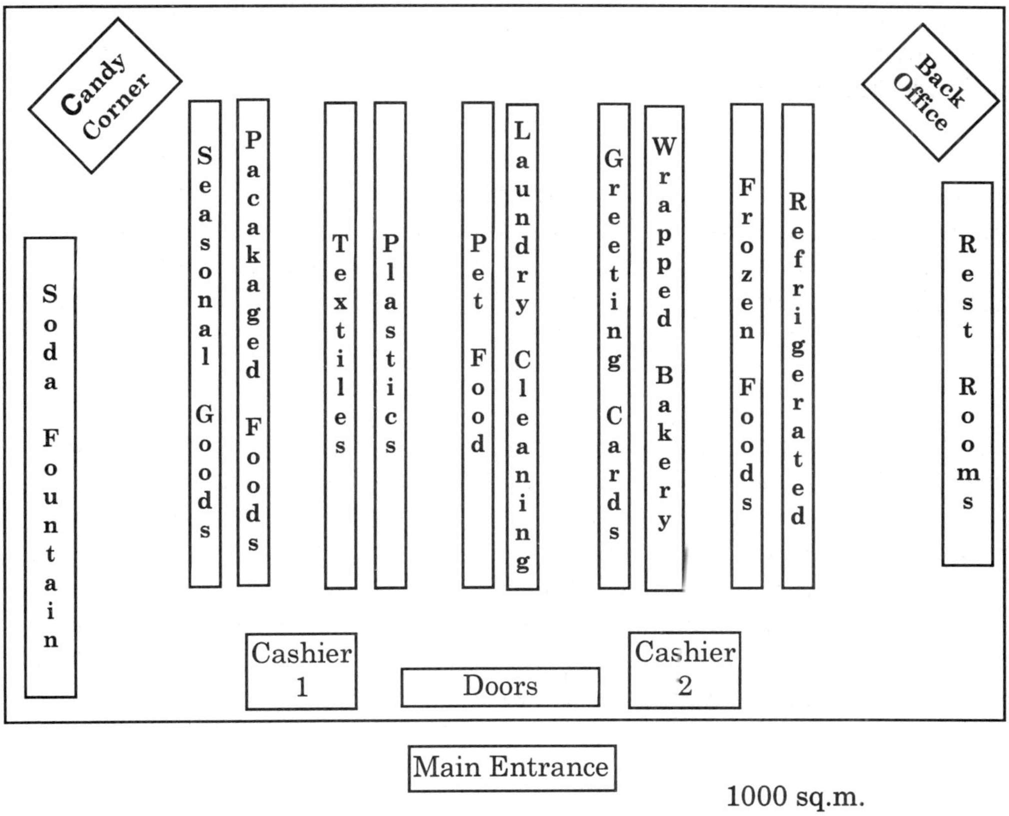

McCARTHY'S NICKEL AND DIME STORE
Case Background

TOWN OF DEERWATER, KANSAS

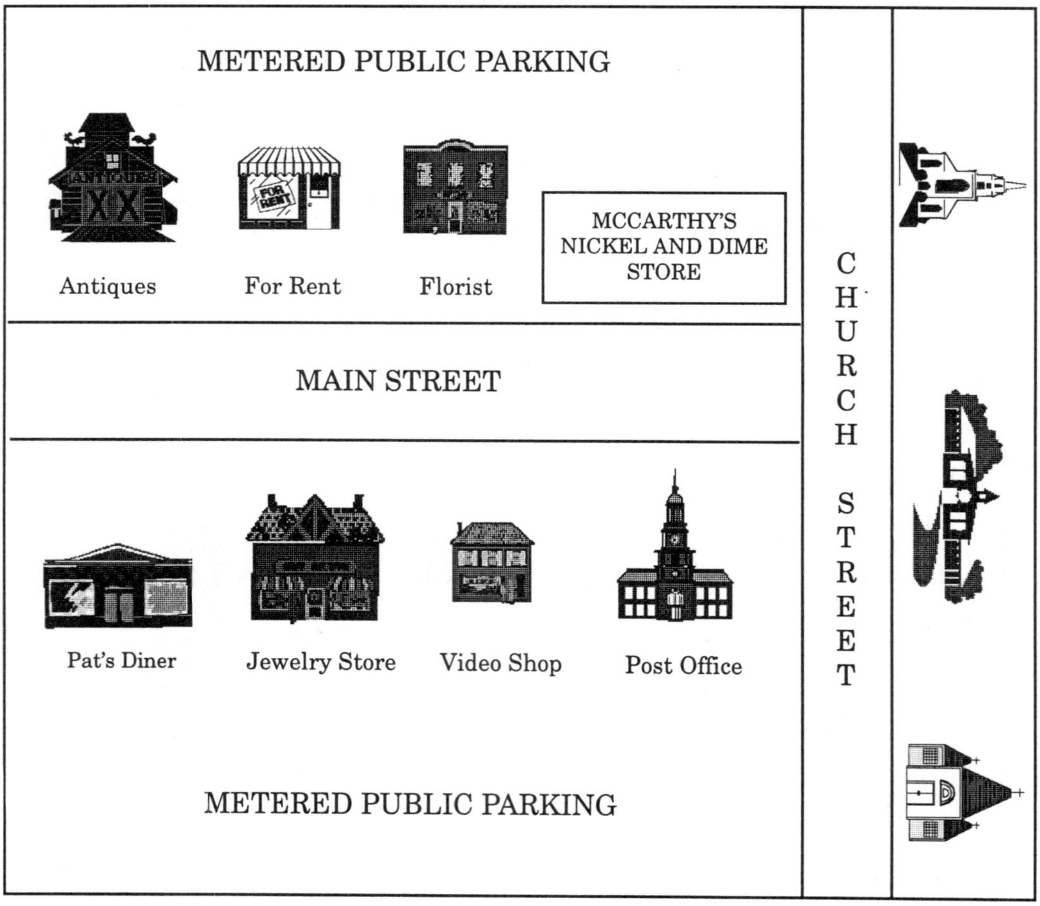

McCarthy's Nickel and Dime Store
Case Background

INFORMATION ON DEERWATER KANSAS

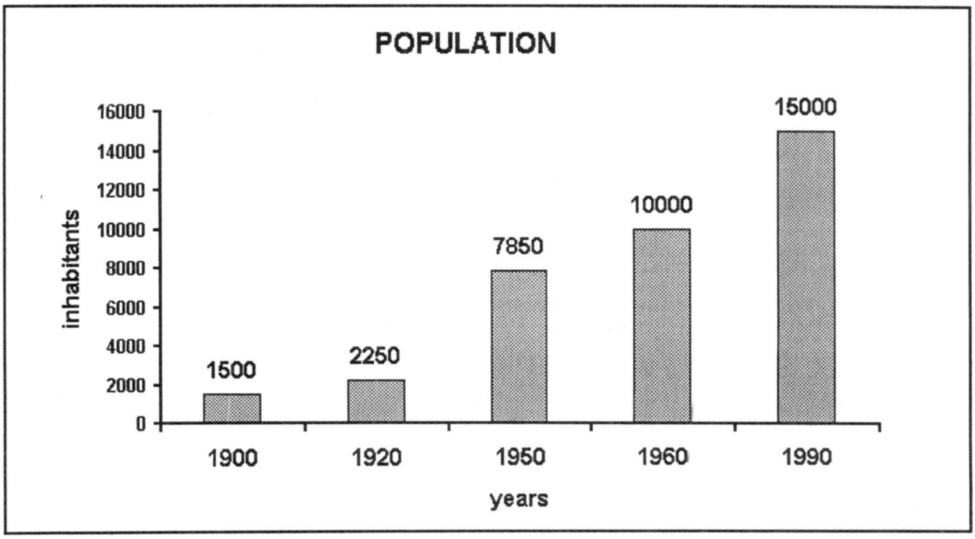

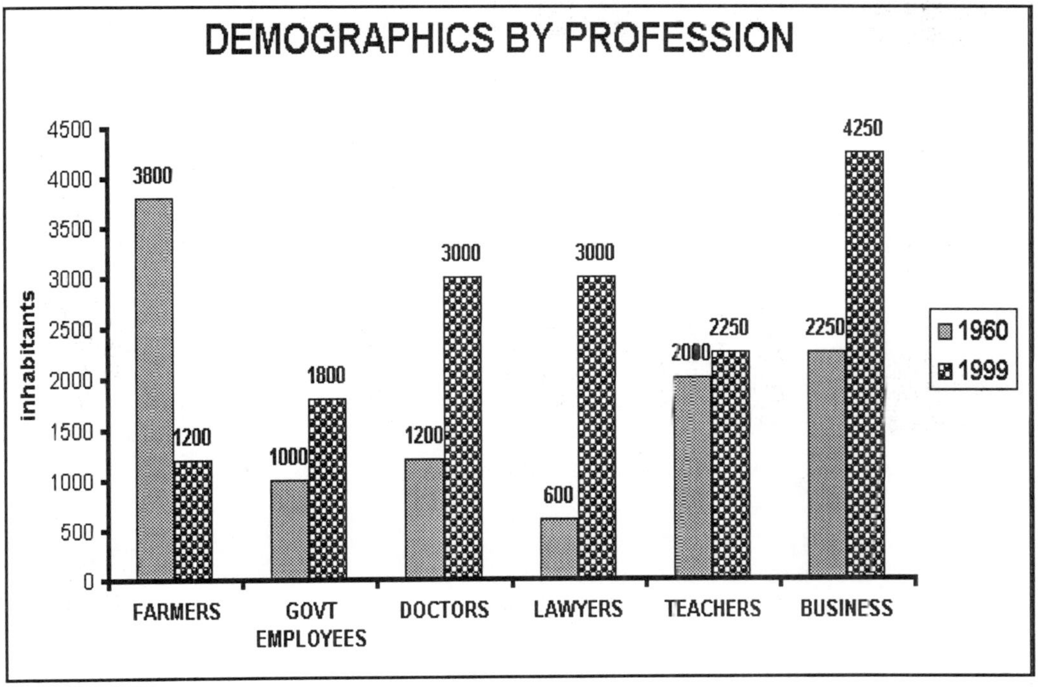

McCARTHY'S NICKEL AND DIME STORE
Application Exercises

ASSIGNMENT

You are Sean McCarthy, the eldest grandson, to whom the business has been bequeathed. You wish to take an active role in the future of the company and continue the McCarthy Nickel and Dime Store tradition. Essential information about the store's current situation will need to be studied and can be found in the case materials and exhibits:

1. the location and layout of the store including some merchandising information
2. inventory and profit margins made within the last six months
3. Deerwater and its demographics
4. the balance sheet from last year
5. the employees, their salaries and their tasks
6. a recent article about a Deerwater megastore

Using this information, address the store's predicament in a 15 minute oral exposé with visuals, a written summary of no more than 400 words, and a drawing or explanation of any new merchandising policies.

Before you begin, you should study the definitions which follow (Exercise 1) and answer the questions (Exercise 2) and carefully study the exhibits.

DIRECTIONS FOR EXERCISE 1

Word choice: retail price; depreciation; overheads; accounts receivable; revenues; materials/wholesale items.

1. Store revenues are calculted by multiplying the ___________ by the number of units sold

2. Cost of Goods Sold reflects the price of obtaining __________ to make the product available.

3. Gross Profit is obtained by subtracting the costs of goods sold from ___________.

4. Operating Expenses includes ____________ such as utilities, but also salaries and interest. It reflects administrative expenses too.

5. ______________ refers to equipment which loses value over time.

6. The sum of cash, inventory, and incoming paid debts is referred to as ____________________.

McCarthy's Nickel and Dime Store Application Exercises

DIRECTIONS FOR EXERCISE 2

Answer the following questions in full sentences by making references to the case materials.

A. STORE LAYOUT AND LOCATION

1. How does a store's layout have an impact on sales?
2. What traditional features might be maintained in McCarthy's?
3. What renovations are absolutely necessary?
4. Should items be shifted around in the store?
5. Draw up a new floor plan for the store.
6. Do the surrounding stores change any of the stock decisions?

B. PROFIT AND LOSS STATEMENT/BALANCE SHEET

1. Judging from the information given, can you evaluate the financial position of McCarthy's?
2. What figures need further explanation?
3. Where do budget cuts seem most vital?
4. What information would help complete the financial picture of McCarthy's?

C. INVENTORY STATEMENT

1. Which aisles seem most profitable?
2. Why maintain non-profitable products?
3. How can customer demand be evaluated by using these tables?
4. Are there areas where money is clearly being lost?
5. What areas might earn more?

McCARTHY'S NICKEL AND DIME STORE
Exhibit 1

ITEM	WHOLE-SALE PRICE	RETAIL PRICE	MARGIN UNIT	MARK-UP(%)
SODA FOUNTAIN				
McCarthy's Soda	1	2,5	1,5	60
Colas	0.75	2,25	1,5	66,66
Lemonades	0.50	1,5	1	66,66
Coffee and Tea	0.50	1,5	1	66,66
SESONAL GOODS				
Decorations	2.75	5,5	2,75	50
Plastic Cups and Plates	2.25	5,25	3	57,14
Toys	6.50	12,12	5,62	46,36
PACKAGE FOODS				
Soup	0.50	1,75	1,25	71,42
Cake mix	1.25	2,5	1,25	50
Flour	0.75	2	1,25	62,5
Sugar	1.59	3,29	1,7	51,67
Bread Crumbs	0.99	2,59	1,6	61,77
TEXTILES				
Bath Towels	2.50	5,25	2,75	52,38
Kitchen Towels	3.50	8,25	4,75	57,57
Curtains	12.50	23,99	11,49	47,89
Throw Rugs	9.99	21,99	12	54,57
PLASTICS				
Plastic Kitchenware	0.59	1,39	0,8	57,55
Thermos	1.59	3,39	1,8	53,09
Buckets	0.99	2,39	1,4	58,57
PET SUPPLIES				
Cat Litter	5.00	11,99	6,99	58,29
Cat food	0.99	2,39	1,4	58,57
Dog food	0.99	2,39	1,4	58,57
Canary food	0.59	1,79	1,2	67,03
Hamster food	0.59	1,39	1,2	67,03
Fish food	0.59	1,39	1,2	67,03
LAUNDRY/CLEANING				
Kitchen Cleaning	1.19	2,69	1,5	55,76
Bathroom Cleaning	1.19	2,59	1,5	55,76
Soaps	0.99	3,29	2,3	69,9
Laundry Detergent	1.99	4,79	2,8	58,45

McCarthy's Nickel and Dime Store
Exhibit 1 (cont)

ITEM	WHOLE-SALE PRICE	RETAIL PRICE	MARGIN UNIT	MARK-UP(%)
PHARMACY				
Cold/Cough Medecine	3.29	7,99	4,7	58,82
Aspirin/Sinus	3.29	7,99	4,7	58,82
Bandages	2.00	5,39	3,39	62,89
Tooth paste/brushes	1.19	3,29	2,1	63,82
Diapers/Sanitary	4.99	10,99	6	54,59
Combs, Brushes	1.99	4,39	2,4	54,66
Shampoo	2.39	5,39	3	55,65
GREETING CARDS				
Birthday	1.50	4,5	3	66,66
Anniversary	1.50	4,5	3	66,66
Sympathy	1.50	4,5	3	66,66
Baptism	1.50	4,5	3	66,66
WRAPPED/BAKERY				
Cookies	1.29	2,39	1,1	46,02
Cakes	1.29	2,39	1,1	46,02
White Bread	1.59	1,59	0	0
Whole Wheat Bread	1.69	1,69	0	0
Pita	1.29	1,29	0	0
FROZEN FOODS				
Vegetables	0.99	1,79	0,8	44,69
French Fries	0.99	1,79	0,8	44,69
Pizza	2.19	5,89	3,7	62,81
Bread/Baked	0.99	1,79	0,8	44,69
Juices	0.99	2,39	1,4	58,57
DAIRY/REFRIGERATED				
Milk	0.99	0,99	0	0
Skim Milk	1.09	1,69	0,6	35,5
Butter/Margarine	2.29	2,29	0	0
Cream	1.59	2,29	0,7	30,56
Juice	1.99	1,99	0	0
Yoghurt	0.69	1,09	0,4	36,69
jarred fish	1.09	3,29	2,2	66,86
ham	2.29	2,59	0,3	11,58
cheese	3.29	3,99	0,7	17,54

McCARTHY'S NICKEL AND DIME STORE
Exhibit 2

	QUANTITIES BOUGHT	PURCHASE ($)	QUANTITIES SOLD	PURCHASE PRICE	SALES REVENUE	GROSS PROFIT
SODA FOUNTAIN		25550		23500	65500	42000
McCarthy's Soda	10800	10800	10000	10000	25000	15000
Colas	7000	5250	6000	4500	13500	9000
Lemonades	5000	2500	4000	2000	6000	4000
Coffee and Tea	14000	7000	14000	7000	21000	14000
SEASONAL GOODS		7200		5400	10497	5097
Decorations	400	1100	300	825	1650	825
Plastic Cups and Plates	400	900	300	675	1575	900
Toys	800	5200	600	3900	7272	3372
PACKAGE FOODS		5080		3926	9256	5330
Soup	1000	500	800	400	1400	1000
Cake mix	1000	1250	800	1000	2000	1000
Flour	1000	750	800	600	1600	1000
Sugar	1000	1590	900	1431	2961	1530
Bread Crumbs	1000	990	500	495	1295	800
TEXTILES		32392		23945	51640	27695
Bath Towels	2400	6000	2000	5000	10500	5500
Kitchen Towels	2400	8400	2200	7700	18150	10450
Curtains	800	10000	500	6250	11995	5745
Throw Rugs	800	7992	500	4995	10995	6000
PLASTICS		3183		1988,3	4593,3	2605
Plastic Kitchenware	2400	1416	2100	1239	2919	1680
Thermos	800	1272	300	477	1017	540
Buckets	500	495	275	272,25	657,25	385
PET SUPPLIES		17460		14255	34355	20100
Cat Litter	2400	12000	2000	10000	23980	13980
Cat food	2400	2376	2000	1980	4780	2800
Dog food	2400	2376	2000	1980	4780	2800
Canary food	400	236	300	177	537	360
Hamster food	400	236	100	59	139	80
Fish food	400	236	100	59	139	80
LAUNDRY/CLEANING		8040		6830	16990	10160
Kitchen Cleaning	1500	1785	1200	1428	3228	1800
Bathroom Cleaning	1500	1785	1200	1428	3108	1680
Soaps	1500	1485	1200	1188	3948	2760
Laundry Detergent	1500	2985	1400	2786	6706	3920

McCarthy's Nickel and Dime Store
Exhibit 2 (cont)

	QUANTITIES BOUGHT	PURCHASE ($)	QUANTITIES SOLD	PURCHASE PRICE	SALES REVENUE	GROSS PROFIT
PHARMACY		24525		18812	44120	25308
Cold/Cough Medecine	1500	4935	1200	3948	9588	5640
Aspirin/Sinus	1500	4935	1200	3948	9588	5640
Bandages	800	1600	200	400	1078	678
Tooth paste/brushes	1000	1190	900	1071	2961	1890
Diapers/Sanitary	1500	7485	1350	6736.5	14837	8100
Combs, Brushes	1000	1990	400	796	1756	960
Shampoo	1000	2390	800	1912	4312	2400
GREETING CARDS		6000		2775	8325	5550
Birthday	1000	1500	600	900	2700	1800
Anniversary	1000	1500	700	1050	3150	2100
Sympathy	1000	1500	400	600	1800	1200
Baptism	1000	1500	150	225	675	450
WRAPPED/BAKERY		23182		18425	22605	4180
Cookies	2400	3096	1800	2322	4302	1980
Cakes	2400	3096	2000	2580	4780	2200
White Bread	4000	6360	3000	4770	4770	0
Whole Wheat Bread	4000	6760	3500	5915	5915	0
Pita	3000	3870	2200	2838	2838	0
FROZEN FOODS		6150		4248	9898	5650
Vegetables	1000	990	400	396	716	320
French Fries	1000	990	400	396	716	320
Pizza	1000	2190	900	1971	5301	3330
Bread/Baked	1000	990	700	693	1253	560
Juices	1000	990	800	792	1912	1120
DAIRY/REFRIGERATED		42691		32515	40395	7880
Milk	5000	4950	4200	4158	4158	0
Skim Milk	2000	2180	1600	1744	2704	960
Butter/Margarine	3000	6870	1500	3435	3435	0
Cream	1500	2385	1200	1908	2748	840
Juice	3000	5970	2400	4776	4776	0
Yoghurt	3000	2070	2600	1794	2834	1040
Jarred fish	1400	1526	1200	1308	3948	2640
Ham	3000	6870	2400	5496	6216	720
Cheese	3000	9870	2400	7896	9576	1680
TOTAL		201453		156619	318174	161555

McCARTHY'S NICKEL AND DIME STORE
Exhibit 3

	INVENTORY	INVENTORY ($)	LOSSES (QTY)	LOSSES (PRICE)	NET PROFIT
SODA FOUNTAIN		2000	800	550	41450
McCarthy's Soda	600	600	200	200	14800
Colas	800	600	200	150	8850
Lemonades	800	400	200	100	3900
Coffee and Tea	800	400	200	100	13900
SEASONAL GOODS		1430		77,5	5019,5
Decorations	100	275	0	0	825
Plastic Cups and Plates	80	180	20	45	855
Toys	150	975	50	32,5	3339,5
PACKAGE FOODS		926,75		227,25	5102,75
Soup	100	50	100	50	950
Cake mix	150	187,5	50	62,5	937,5
Flour	100	75	100	75	925
Sugar	75	119,25	25	39,75	1490,25
Bread Crumbs	500	495	0	0	800
TEXTILES		9021		2049	25646
Bath Towels	300	750	100	250	5250
Kitchen Towels	150	525	50	175	10275
Curtains	300	3750	50	625	5120
Throw Rugs	400	3996	100	999	5001
PLASTICS		993,8		101,95	2503,05
Plastic Kitchenware	250	147,5	50	29,5	1650,5
Thermos	470	747,3	30	47,7	492,3
Buckets	100	99	25	24,75	360,25
PET SUPPLIES		2841,25		363,75	19736,25
Cat Litter	350	1750	50	250	13730
Cat food	350	346,5	50	49,5	2750,5
Dog food	350	346,5	50	49,5	2750,5
Canary food	75	44,25	25	14,75	345,25
Hamster food	300	177	0	0	80
Fish food	300	177	0	0	80
LAUNDRY/CLEANING		962		248	9912
Kitchen Cleaning	200	238	100	119	1681
Bathroom Cleaning	275	327,25	25	29,75	1650,25
Soaps	250	247,5	50	49,5	2710,5
Laundry Detergent	75	149,25	25	49,75	3870,25

	INVENTORY	INVENTORY ($)	LOSSES (QTY)	LOSSES (PRICE)	NET PROFIT
PHARMACY		5180,75		1190,55	24117,45
Cold/Cough Medecine	200	658	100	329	5311
Aspirin/Sinus	200	658	100	329	5311
Bandages	550	1100	50	100	578
Tooth paste/brushes	80	952	20	23,8	1866,2
Diapers/Sanitary	100	499	50	249,5	7850,5
Combs, Brushes	450	895,5	50	99,5	860,5
Shampoo	175	418,25	25	59,75	2340,25
GREETING CARDS		2932,5		292,5	5257,5
Birthday	325	487,5	75	112,5	1687,5
Anniversary	230	345	70	105	1995
Sympathy	575	862,5	25	37,5	1162,5
Baptism	825	1237,5	25	37,5	412,5
WRAPPED/BAKERY		1553,5		3203,5	976,5
Cookies	550	709,5	50	64,5	1915,5
Cakes	300	387	100	129	2071
White Bread	100	159	900	1431	-1431
Whole Wheat Bread	100	169	400	676	-676
Pita	100	129	700	903	-903
FROZEN FOODS		1363,2		439,8	5210,2
Vegetables	300	297	200	198	122
French Fries	600	594	0	0	320
Pizza	80	175,2	20	43,8	3286,2
Bread/Baked	150	148,5	150	148,5	411,5
Juices	150	148,5	50	49,5	1070,5
DAIRT/REFRIGERATED		6161		4015	3865
Milk	600	594	200	198	-198
Skim Milk	300	327	100	109	851
Butter/Margarine	1000	2290	500	1145	-1145
Cream	250	397,5	50	79,5	760,5
Juice	300	597	300	597	-597
Yoghurt	250	172,5	150	103,5	936,5
jarred fish	100	109	100	109	2531
ham	300	687	300	687	33
cheese	300	987	300	987	693
TOTAL		35365,75		12758,85	148795,6

McCarthy's Nickel and Dime Store
Balance Sheet Exhibit 3

ASSETS

Current Assets		
Cash		25,465.00
Accounts Receivable	12,787.55	
Less Doubtful Accounts -	$2,500	10,287.55
Merchandise Inventory		35,366.00
Prepaid Expenses		21,396.00
Total Current Assets		92,514.55
Fixed Assets		
Land		28,000.00
Building		82,316.00
Less Accumulated Depreciation		15,000.00
Equipment		25,000.00
Less Accumulated Depreciation		15,000.00
Total Fixed Assets		105,316.45
Intangible Assets		
Goodwill		20,000.00
Patent		5,000.00
Trademark		25,000.00
Total Intangible Assets		50,000.00
TOTAL ASSETS		**247,831.00**

McCarthy's Nickel and Dime Store
Balance Sheet

LIABILITIES AND OWNER'S EQUITY

Current Liabilities	
Accounts payable	21,794.58
Wages payable	91,500.00
Taxes payable	6,852.34
Total Current Liabilities	**120,146.92**
Long Term Liabilities	
Notes payable 8% 1996 (heating installation)	10,526.23
Total Long Term Liabilities	10,526.23
TOTAL LIABILITIES	**130,673.15**
Owner's Equity	
Common Stock $5 par	20,000.00
Additional paid-in capital	.00
Retained earnings	97,157.85
TOTAL OWNER'S EQUITY	**117,157.85**
TOTAL LIABILITIES AND OWNER'S EQUITY	**247,831.00**

McCarthy's Nickel and Dime Store
Income Statement Exhibit 5

McCarthy's Nickel and Dime Store
1134 Clearview Highway
Deerwater, KA 92456-0987
USA

McCarthy's Nickel and Dime Store.
Income Statement
Year ended, December 31st, 1998

REVENUES (gross sales)	**$318,174.00**
Cost of goods sold:	
Merchandise inventory January 1st 1998	25,743.00
Merchandise purchases during the year	201,453.00
Goods available for sale	
Less: Merchandise inventory December 31st 1998	-$35,366.00
Cost of goods sold	**$191,830.00**
GROSS PROFIT	**$126,344.00**
Operating expenses:	
Selling and repackaging expenses:	
Advertising	2,345
Depreciation - warehouse equipment	1,350
Delivery service (truck and packaging)	1,672
Administrative expenses:	
Salaries and wages	91,500
Supplies	6,589
Utilities	4,800
Depreciation office and store equipment	2,345
Interest expense	
Miscellaneous expenses	2,942
TOTAL	**$113,543**
Operating income (income before taxes)	$12,801.00
Income and Property Taxes	-$2,369.00
NET INCOME	**$10,432.00**

McCarthy's Nickel and Dime Store
Exhibit 6

EMPLOYEE DATA SHEET

Marlene Dwight, 52
Cashier
Started 1990
Part-Time $4,500

Trudy Finn, 48
Accountant
Full time $22,000

Pierce McCarthy, 59
Manager/Buyer
Full Time $27,000

Sean McCarthy, 27
Stock Clerk
Full Time $13,000

Kate Smith, 25
Cashier
Part Time $4,000

Joe Speerwater, 53
Janitor
Full Time $13,000

Tennessee Wyatt, 47
Soda Jerk
Part Time $8,000

TOTAL $91,500 Annual Salary

McCarthy's Nickel and Dime Store is an equal opportunity employer

Cultural Facts You Should Consider

Some products are sold at a loss in certain stores in order to guarantee a steady flow of customers for staple items. It is hoped that impulse purchasing will compensate.

The American General Store originated in small towns and was first designed to stock every imaginable item for sale - from gunpower to girdles, from parakeets to turtles.

The soda fountain is also an American tradition. Serving non-alchoholic beverages and sometimes ice-cream and coffee, it is the hallmark of small town living.

McCarthy's Nickel and Dime Store
Exhibit 7

The Deerwater Clarion, April 15th, 1999

FLINCHES SUPERMARKETS COMES TO DEERWATER GRAND OPENING THIS SUNDAY

The chain of large supermarkets called Flinches, in an effort to further expand in the heartland, has opened up 15 new megastores in the state of Kansas. Serving the town of Deerwater, the new store is located on Route 19, just south of the Old Oklahoma City Road and two miles from Kansas State 901. Flinches supermarkets has announced their grand opening for this Sunday.

The supermarket will employ over 50 local people full-time. Over 30 part-time positions at the cash register and in stock have also been created bringing some relief to a community which has been unable to re-employ many of its former farm hands.

Supplying the Deerwater community and its countryside, the supermarket has been planned to supply a population of around 15,000 people of middle-class and upper-middle class backgrounds.

Market surveys have indicated that the Deerwater area has grown in population by 10 percent over the last five years. This is due to the high quality of life the city offers and also to the construction of two new computer processing plants in the Riverview Valley which have brought wealthier executives and their families to the area.

The store offers bargains for staple items and features a gourmet delicatessen, a flower shop, an exotic pet store plus an area for the purchase of books, CD's and newspapers.

We highly recommend their take-out coffee from the gourmet shop!

Heard Around the Town

«Well, it's about time somebody has done something to improve the shopping in Deerwater».
Kay Keyton, 36 years old, mother of 6 children

«It makes no difference at all for people who live in town».
Earl Ready, 85 years old, retired.

«We are grateful to Flinches for their contribution to the community.»
Josey Black, Principal of the Deerwater High School

«Flinches ain't really that cheap».
Anonymous

«My purpose is to protect small business from large scale infiltration of multinationals.» ***Joe Huey, Democratic Representative Deerwater City Council***

COUPON
$15
off the next purchase of an exotic pet
redeemable only at
FLINCHES
Coupon expires May 31st, 2000

COUPON
$2
off the next pharmaceutical purchase
redeemable only at
FLINCHES
Coupon expires May 31st, 2000

COUPON
50c
off Flinches trash bags
redeemable only at
FLINCHES
Coupon expires May 31st, 2000

Answer Key

The following answer key contains solutions only to short answer application exercises. No case solutions or model correspondence is provided for the longer application exercises given the complexity of the contexts and the variety of possible «correct» answers.

THE HABITAT CATALOGUE COMPETITION

Exercise 4

1. the subject
2. introducing, will, present
3. explained, our, onto
4. how
5. loyalty, objectives
6. date
7. dealt, issues, consider, deadlines
8. loss leader, takes, concern, pricing
9. divided, parts
10. overstated, criticised, aspired to
11. sustained/captured, persuasive
12. considering/examining discussing/questioning
13. counterfeiting, bear, mass, in
14. after
15. told, you, said, suggestion

STARTING A NEW COMPANY

Exercise 5

1. on account of
2. in spite of
3. for the purpose of
4. whereas
5. to the extent that
6. obviously
7. Judging from these examples
8. thus

VAN HAFFNER TOYS

Exercise 2

1. trade creditors
2. accounts receivable
3. share capital
4. tax accounting period
5. net income
6. profit and loss account
7. inventory
8. stocks
9. bills
10. net worth
11. quoted investments
12. accruals

VAN HAFFNER TOYS

Exercise 3

ITEM	SELF-TEST
1. retained earnings	G
2. current assets	C
3. corporation tax	A
4. fixed assets	E
5. current liabilities	D
6. depreciation	B
7. net working capital	F
8. long-term debt	H

McCARTHY'S NICKEL AND DIME STORE

Exercise 1

1. retail price
2. wholesale items
3. revenues
4. overheads
5. depreciation
6. accounts receivable

Glossary

This glossary lists only items used in the manual. Each entry is followed by a short French translation and a second meaning is given for words that may present certain ambiguities. Priority is given to the meaning most relevant to the context in which it is used in this book.

Abreviations Used

n. noun
v. verb
adj. adjective
adv. adverb
exp. fixed expression i.e., the words taken separately mean something different
pl. plural

A

accounting (n.) comptabilité
accounts payable (US) (n.) dettes passives ou fournisseurs
accounts receivable (n.) compte client ou débiteur
accounts receivable (US) (n.) créances clients
accruals (n.) charges à payer
accrued expenses (n.) charges à payer
acknowledged (adj.) reconnu
aisles (n.) bas-côté, allée
alimony (n.) pension alimentaire
allowance (n.) indemnité
anticipate (v.) prévenir, prévoir, voir par avance
applicant (n.) candidat
appraisal (n.) appréciation, évaluation
articulate (adv.) exprimé clairement
assertive (adj.) qui avance ses idées facilement
assets (n.) actif

B

balance sheet (n.) bilan
bank charges (n.) agios
bank fees (n.) frais bancaires
bear in mind (v.) tenir compte de
bequeath (v.) léguer, transmettre
bet, You bet ! (exp.) Tu parles !
bill of exchange (n.) traite, effet de commerce
bill payable (n.) effet à payer
bill receivable (n.) effet à recevoir
bolster (v.) renforcer
bond (n.) action
brigade, (n.) one of the old brigade (exp.) un vétéran, un vieux de la vieille
building (n.) bâtiment
buyout (n.) rachat

C

call for tender (v.) soumissionner
cash (n.) argent liquide
cash flow (n.) trésorerie
chain of command (exp.) voie hiérarchique
cheerful (adj.) attrayant
collateral (n.) nantissement, caution
commercial paper (n.) effets de commerce
common carrier (n.) entreprise de transport
common stock (US) (n.) actions ordinaires
company policy (n.) politique de l'entreprise
compassionate (adj.) compatissant
competitive edge (exp.) avance sur la concurrence
conceit (n.) vanité, prétention
concern for (n.) préoccupation avec
considerate (adj.) prévenant
constant stream (exp.) flot continu
consumer market (exp) marché de la consommation
corporate culture (exp.) culture d'entreprise
corporation tax (n.) impôt sur les sociétés
cost accounting (n.) comptabilité analytique
cost of goods sold (exp.) coût des marchandises vendues
cost overrun (n.) dépassement des coûts
cost-effective (adj.) rentable
counterfeit (n.) contrefaçon
coupon (n.) bon de réduction
credit rating (n.) statut financier
creditors (GB) (n.) dettes fournisseurs
creditworthiness (n.) solvabilité
current assets (n.) actif circulant, réalisable
current liabilities (n.) passif exigible, dettes à court terme
curtain (n.) rideau
customer service (n.) service clientèle

D

debenture (n.) dette à long terme (GB), obligation non garantie
debtors (GB) (n.) créances clients
decisive (adj.) décidé, catégorique
deferred taxes (n.) impôts à payer
departmentalization (n.) organisation en départements
depreciation (n.) amortissement
diaper (n.) couche-culotte (US) nappy (GB)
disc submission (exp.) proposition sur disquette
discount a bill (v.) escompter une traite
DIY shop (Do-it-yourself shop) (exp.) magasin de bricolage

dovetail (v.) s'intégrer
downsize (v.) réduire les effectifs de
draw a bill (v.) tirer une traite
draw up (v.) dresser, établir
draw up a balance-sheet (v.) établir un bilan
drive (n.) énergie, dynamisme
due date (exp.) échéance

E

easy-going (adj.) accommodant
enhance (v.) mettre en valeur
enter an item (v.) passer une écriture
equities (n.) actions ordinaires
equity capital (n.) capital actions
expenses (n.) dépenses
experience (n.) pratique, expérience
experiment (n.) expérience, essai
extraordinary profit (or loss) (n.) bénéfice (ou perte) exceptionnel

F

facilitator (n.) facilitateur, animateur
fall due (v.) échoir, venir à échéance
fall through (v.) échouer
financial year (GB) (n.) exercice
finished goods (n.) produits finis
finishes (n.) finitions
fiscal year (US) (n.) exercice
fixed assets (n.) actif immobilisé
flaunt (v.) étaler, afficher, faire étalage de
forecast (v.) prévoir
forefront (n.) au premier rang de
free-lance (adj.) indépendant
fund-raising (n.) collecte de fonds

G

get back to (v.) recontacter qn
give the go-ahead (for sth) (v.) donner le feu vert
Goldsmiths (n.) une prestigieuse école d'art (University of London)
grant a loan (v.) accorder un prêt
Great stuff ! (exp.) Bien joué! (langage parlé)
greeting card (n.) carte de voeux
gross operating profit (n.) excédent brut d'exploitation
gross profit (n.) bénéfice brut
guarantee (n.) caution, cautionnement, couverture
guideline (n.) ligne directrice

H

handle (v.) mener
hands-on (exp.) « sur le tas », pratique
hang around (v.) attendre
headquarter (n.) siège social
heartland (n.) le mid-ouest américain
hectic (adj.) intense, terrible
high-flyer (exp.) personne qui fait carrière de manière fulgurante
humdrum (adj.) monotone, banal, routinier
hunch (n.) intuition, pressentiment

I

I.P.O. (Initial Public Offering) (n.) introduction en bourse
in bulk (exp.) en gros
income (n.) revenu
income statement (US) (n.) compte de résultats
inroad (n.) incursion
insight into (n.) aperçu, idée de
insightful (adj.) perspicace
insolvency (n.) insolvabilité
instalments (n.) versements échelonnés
intangible assets (n.) immobilisations incorporelles
interest (n.) intérêt
inventories (US) (n.) stocks
issue (v.) émettre

J

jar (n.) pot
job security (n.) sécurité de l'emploi
job sharing (n.) partage de poste

K

kidding (I was only kidding) ! (exp.) J'ai dit ça pour plaisanter !
knowledgeably (adv.) en toute connaissance

L

L.I.F.O. (Last in First Out) (exp.) dernier entré, premier sorti (DEPS)
lay off (v.) licencier
layoff (n.) licenciement
leasing (n.) crédit-bail, leasing
liabilities (n.) passif, dettes
life cycle (exp.) cycle de vie
line of credit (n.) ligne de crédit

liquid assets (n.) liquidités
lively (adj.) vif, plein d'entrain, pétulant
loan (n.) prêt, emprunt, avance
loan (n.) emprunt
long-term liabilities (n.) dettes à long terme
loss leader (exp.) produit d'appel (vendu à perte pour attirer les clients)

M

make it (v.) y arriver
manufacturing (n.) fabrication, industrie
marketable securities (US) (n.) titres négociables
maturity (n.) échéance, date d'échéance
memorabilia (n.) souvenirs
merger (n.) fusion
meter (n.) parcmètre
mission statement (exp.) définition de mission
mull over (v.) réfléchir à

N

net operating profit (n.) résultat net d'exploitation
net profit after tax (n.) bénéfice net après impôt
net working capital (n.) besoin en fonds de roulement
net worth (n.) capitaux propres
networker (n.) quelqu'un qui se fait des relations
notes payable (n.) effets à payer

O

ordinary shares (GB) (n.) actions ordinaires
outgoing (adj.) ouvert
outplacement (n.) aide à la recherche d'un nouvel emploi fournie par l'employeur lors d'un licenciement
overdraft (n.) découvert
overdraw an account (v.) mettre un compte à découvert
overdue (adj.) arriéré, en retard
overflow (v.) déborder
overheads (n.) frais généraux
overstate (v.) exagérer
overwhelm (v.) submerger
owners' equity (n.) capitaux propres

P

pace (v.) rythme
panel (n.) commission
patent (n.) brevet
pay back (v.) rembourser
persistent (adj.) persévérant
pet supplies (n.) produits pour animaux
phoney (adj.) poseur, pas franc
placement (n.) stage, placement
plant (n.) installations industrielles
plateau (v.) atteindre un palier, se stabiliser, «plafonner»
plough back (v.) réinvestir
position (n.) poste, emploi
prepaid expenses (n.) charges payées d'avance
pre-requisite (adj.) préalablement nécessaire
prioritize (v.) donner la priorité à
profit and loss account (GB) (n.) compte de résultats
profitability (n.) rentabilité
promissory note (n.) billet à ordre
promote (v.) promouvoir
promotion (n.) promotion, avancement
push out (v.) évincer, se débarrasser de
put up money (v.) financer

Q

quoted investments (GB) (n.) titres négociables

R

raise a loan (v.) obtenir un prêt
raise capital (v.) collecter, trouver des capitaux
rank (v.) classer
rear (v.) dresser
redeemable (adj.) remboursable
refund a loan (v.) rembourser un prêt
register (n.) registre
registered trademark (n.) marque déposée
relocate (v.) transférer, muter
report to (v.) dépendre de quelqu'un
reserves (n.) réserves
resourceful (adj.) ingénieux
retail (n.) détail, grande distribution
retail (n., adj.) vente au détail
retail outlet (n.) magasin de détail
retained earnings (n.) bénéfices réinvestis
revenues (n.) recettes
ROI Return On Investment (n.) retour sur investissement
runner-up (n.) second

S

saddle v(adj.) à cheval
screen doors (n.) portes moustiquaires
secured credit, loan (n.) prêt sur garantie

security (n.) caution, cautionnement, garantie
seed money (n.) capital initial, mise de fonds initiale
semi-finished goods (exp.) produits semi-finis
set up (v.) installer
severance pay (n.) indemnité de licenciement
share capital (n.) capital social
shareholder (GB) (n.) actionnaire
shelves (n.) rayons
shift (n.) changement
shortcoming (n.) défaut
shortlist (v.) préselectionner
short-list (n.) présélection
shun (v.) éviter, esquiver
sick pay (n.) indemnité de maladie
sign-off (n.) conclusion
silent partner (n.) commanditaire, bailleur de fonds
sizable (adj.) assez important, assez considérable
skill (n.) savoir, compétence
soda fountain (n.) un bar pour boissons non alcoolisées
solvency (n.) solvabilité
sound judgment (exp.) de bon sens
spread sheets (n.) tableaux, base de données
stand back (v.) s'écarter, prendre du recul
stand out for (v.) se faire remarquer par
staple item (n.) produit de première nécessité
stint (n.) un bref passage
stock (US) (n.) actions
stockholder (US) (n.) actionnaire
stockholders' equity (n.) capitaux propres
stocks (GB) (n.) stocks
streamline (v.) rationaliser, dégraisser
strive for (v.) s'efforcer de, faire son possible pour
stultifying (adj.) abrutissant, déshumanisant
subcontractor (n.) sous-traitant
sustain (attention) (v.) soutenir, maintenir (l'attention)

T

take out a loan (v.) contracter un emprunt
take the floor (v.) prendre la parole
take-off (n.) démarrage
takeover (n.) rachat d'une société
takeover bid (n.) offre publique d'achat
target (n.) but, objectif
tax deductible (adj.) déductible de l'impôt
think tank (n.) groupe de réflexion
thorough (adj.) consciencieux, qui travaille avec beaucoup de rigueur
top-heavy (adj.) trop lourd du haut
towel (n.) serviette
trend (n.) tendance
trump (n.) atout
turnover (n.) chiffre d'affaires

U

unceasing (adj.) incessant, continuel
underwrite (v.) souscrire
undisclosed (adj.) non révélé
unsecured credit (n.) crédit en blanc
untapped (adj.) inexploité
upgrading (n.) amélioration de la qualité
upmarket (n.) évolution vers le haut de gamme
utilities (n.) l'eau, le gaz, l'électricité

V

valuation (n.) valorisation
venture capital (n.) capital-risque
vineyard (n.) vignoble

W

warehouse (n.) entrepôt, magasin
willingly (adv.) volontiers, de bon coeur
work out (v.) élaborer, mettre au point
working capital (n.) fonds de roulement
Work-In-Progress (exp.) travaux en cours
write down (v.) amortir
write off (v.) amortir

Achevé d'imprimer en juillet 2001 dans les ateliers de Normandie Roto Impression s.a., 61250 Lonrai
N° d'impression : 011729 Dépôt légal : juillet 2001